Praise for *Life*

In *Life Change* my friend Jordan Easley guides us through Mark's Gospel with a focus on personal transformation. *Life Change* will make you uncomfortable with where you are while providing clarity about where you need to be.

Andy Stanley
Pastor, North Point Community Church

You really can change! That is the clear affirmation given by Jordan Easley in *Life Change*. Read this book and discover the reality of spiritual transformation now and forever.

Jack Graham
Pastor, Prestonwood Baptist Church

If you're looking for a self-help book, this is not it! But if you're looking for true life transformation offered by an all-powerful, all-loving, all-knowing God, then this book is for you. In these chapters, Jordan inspires and equips us to rely on God for transformation that only He can give.

David Nasser
Pastor, Christ City Church
Author of *Jumping Through Fires, Glory Revealed, The Call, A Call to Grace, A Call to Die,* and other books

As Jordan has faithfully served churches and people, he has seen from the front row the transformation that Jesus brings to the lives of people who trust Him. In *Life Change,* Jordan offers practical insight on personal life change with the understanding that true transformation is always and only rooted in the grace of God.

Eric Geiger
Vice President, LifeWay Christian Resources

Life Change brilliantly shows that it's never too late for a person to change. Nobody is exempt! Change is possible only because of the supernatural power of God, and as we point our feet toward Jesus and walk to Him, we can experience life change firsthand! *Life Change* is a great book of hope!

Johnny Hunt
Senior Pastor, First Baptist Church, Woodstock, Georgia
Former President, Southern Baptist Convention

Are you searching for something different? Looking for something new in your life? Read *Life Change*! It will help you navigate to the future that God wants for you. I believe in Jordan Easley. I believe in *Life Change*!

Ronnie Floyd
Author and Senior Pastor, Cross Church

Life Change is written in simple, user-friendly terms people of every age will enjoy. Jordan Easley addresses the challenge of life change with a step-by-step practical approach, centered on Jesus Christ, the true change agent. As Jordan so aptly states, "No matter the circumstance, change is possible through Jesus Christ," and this book can provide the catalyst.

H. Edwin Young
Senior Pastor, Second Baptist Houston

Jordan Easley represents a new generation of leaders willing to challenge both the culture and the church with the life-giving truth of God's Word. Jordan's charismatic and creative style effectively meets people where they are today.

Ben Young
Pastor, Second Baptist Houston
Author of *Why Mike's Not a Christian*

Is life change possible? Jordan Easley says yes. But it isn't something you do within your own strength. Jordan uses life situations drawn from the Gospel of Mark to show how Christ can bring about life change. You will be blessed and helped by *Life Change*.

Jerry Vines
Paster-Emeritus, First Baptist Church, Jacksonville, Florida,
Two-time President, Southern Baptist Convention and
President, Jerry Vines Ministies

Only you know what's really going on in your life. If you know there's something you need to change, and you just don't know how to do it, then *Life Change* was written just for you. Whether you need to kick a habit, or if your entire lifestyle needs an overhaul, real change is absolutely possible, and Jordan Easley will help you discover what that looks like.

Pete Wilson
Pastor, Cross Point Church, Nashville, Tennessee
Author of *Plan B* and *Empty Promises*

Jordan Easley is a respected voice in the largest churches in America. In his dynamic book, *Life Change*, Easley presents the case that Christ can change the life of the one who is submitted to the timeless precepts of God's Word.

Jeff Neal
Cofounder and Lead Evangelist, Team Impact

You can change! Jordan Easley connects you to the source that can transform you into the person you were created to be in his powerful new book, *Life Change*.

Kerry Shook
Founding Pastor of Woodlands Church, Houston, Texas
Coauthor of the national best sellers *One Month to Live* and
Love at Last Sight

In a world saturated with self-help books and drowning in a sea of secular humanism comes an essential read for those in need of change. In *Life Change,* my friend Jordan Easley takes us on a journey through the Gospel of Mark, where we interact with characters desperate for transformation. Like all great teachers, Jordan uses the Bible to illuminate our need and also provide clarity to the answer for authentic and lasting change. This book was written for all who are thirsty for change—come to the water and be filled.

Brent Crowe
Speaker and Vice President
of Student Leadership University
Author of *Reimagine: What the World Would Look Like If God Got His Way*

In a society that is constantly looking for a quick fix or any shortcut to change a relationship, reverse a lifetime of unhealthy choices, bail out a business—in essence, a game changer—Jordan Easley provides us with *Life Change*. He wastes no time in getting down to business. The very fact that he uses the Gospel of Mark, the bottom-line action Gospel, is a good indication. Hold your breath, and hang on as you come face-to-face with the truth of God that gives us the courage to face our realities. Don't waste another precious second, because these truths are transformational and, more important, transferable. The stuff in this book still works! If I want to know about coaching, I'm interested in what Lombardi or Landry had to say. If I want to know about character under fire, I'm interested in what Churchill and Lincoln said and did. And if I want to know how to communicate with this generation and empower them to untangle the knots in their life, Jordan Easley is who I want to read.

Jay Strack
President and Founder of Student Leadership University

"Everyone thinks of changing the world, but no one thinks of changing himself." These words by Leo Tolstoy remind us how easy it is to become idealistic about change without considering ourselves. In *Life Change,* Jordan Easley offers practical, biblical help for the person who understands the only way to change the world is to stare in the mirror. You will be encouraged, challenged, and engaged by this book.

Alvin L. Reid, PhD
Professor at Southeastern Baptist Theological Seminary
Author of *As You Go* and *Evangelism Handbook*

Most of us are rarely satisfied with who we are and are constantly fighting for change. Jordan Easley's *Life Change* will help anyone navigate the stages and steps of spiritual change and point to real people who've been through it.

Matt Lawson
Student Pastor, First Baptist Church, Woodstock, Georgia
Author of *Twisdom*

While reading this book, I found Jordan time and time again answering questions that I didn't realize my heart was asking. Every human desires change but we struggle to figure how to make it happen. In this amazingly practical book, Jordan helps us realize and believe that life change is found only in the accessible presence of Christ.

Drew Worsham
Campus Pastor, Resonate Church, Pullman, Washington
Magician/Mentalist

There is no one better to write about life change than Jordan Easley. He has committed his life to allow God to use him to invest in others and see life change take place. You will read in this book a simple, practical approach to life change all centered around God's Word. Jordan shows us how we can all change and unpacks how to allow change to take place. It is a must-read book and a great book to use for discipleship groups, sermon series, or even a small group study.

Brian Mills
Student Pastor, Long Hollow Baptist Church,
Hendersonville, Tennessee
Author of *Checkpoints: A Tactical Guide to Manhood*

Each of us knows, intuitively, that there are both small and big changes we need to make in our lives. Yet we also know that it's much easier to stay as we are, because change is hard. Jordan Easley shows that it's possible, and not as hard as you think, to make those life changes, and he gives you practical, doable steps to get you there, starting with embracing the power of Jesus Christ to change you at your deepest level.

Clayton King
Founder and President, Crossroads Ministries
Teaching Pastor, NewSpring Church

lifechange

JORDAN EASLEY

foreword by Gary Thomas

lifechange

finding a
new way
to **hope,**
think and **live**

B&H
PUBLISHING GROUP

Nashville, Tennessee

Published by B&H Publishing Group, Nashville, Tennessee

Dewey Decimal Classification: 248.84
Subject Heading: CHANGE \ CHRISTIAN LIFE \ BIBLE.
N.T. MARK—STUDY

Published in association with KLO Publishing Service, LLC
(www.KLOPublishing.com)

1 2 3 4 5 6 7 8 • 17 16 15 14 13

I dedicate this book to my Dad, Dr. Ernest Easley—
my hero, mentor, and friend.

I'm grateful that he loved me enough to introduce me to the
life-changing power of Jesus when I was a small boy, and I'm
thankful that he's courageously lived out his faith and modeled
what following Jesus looks like every day of my life.

Contents

Foreword by Gary Thomas xvii

Introduction 1

Chapter 1: Life Change 3

Chapter 2: A Life in Need of Healing 29

Chapter 3: How to Position Your Life for Change 49

Chapter 4: The Touch That Changes Everything 73

Chapter 5: It's Never Too Late for Change 89

Chapter 6: Change That Leads to Freedom 113

Chapter 7: Open Ears, Open Hearts, Changed Lives ... 135

Chapter 8: Change Fighter 151

Chapter 9: Life Change in Practical Terms 167

About the Author 183

Foreword

Growing up in the sixties, we kids often heard, "You should be ashamed of yourself." That phrase has all but disappeared in modern child-rearing—to our society's great detriment. Shame *can* be destructive, but it has a healthy place. We should be fans of healthy shame.

A young man once asked to get together with me when, after a conversation, he knew I was disappointed with his actions. This young man is generally a "good" kid, an earnest believer, and mature in many respects. But he had acted in a dishonorable way. His youth leader had worked patiently to help him see how his actions weren't appropriate, and following that the young man wanted to also meet with me, eager to explain his actions.

I affirmed the youth pastor's concerns; the young man still tried to defend himself by saying, "It just happened."

"That's where you and I disagree," I countered. "It didn't *just happen.* You made several small choices that led to this. In the long run, did you want what happened to happen? No. But your many earlier choices naturally gave birth to what did happen, and that's what you need to accept responsibility for. Somewhere along the way, by your actions, you chose for this to happen."

His mother grew angry with me, saying her son's character was "unassailable." In a world where the Bible says, "we all stumble in many ways" (James 3:2), I'm not sure *anyone's* character is unassailable, much less a teenager who is learning his way in the world. Yet we are so fearful of shame that we act like admitting an error is a greater evil than committing one.

Jordan Easley points us to a different pursuit: Rather than defend our poor character, why not cooperate with God's work, surrender to the Master's touch, and be changed?

Because of grace, I can face those things in my life that need to be changed rather than try to explain them away. For instance, there are times when I let food get the best of me. I can inhale my food with the force of an industrial vacuum, in a way that is rude and, yes, shameful. Just the other day, my wife cut up some fruit and berries while I was watching a football game. Maybe it was the intensity of the moment, but I all but swallowed that bowl of fruit whole, never even really enjoying or tasting it. Lisa walked down the stairs, saw the empty bowl she had just placed in front of me, and her mouth dropped open in astonishment.

I hate it when I do this, and I'm rightly ashamed of it. Afterwards, when I become aware of it, I repent, ask God's forgiveness, and try to be more mindful of it the next time I'm in such a situation.

I don't expect myself—or others—to be perfect. Even mature people can occasionally do shameful things. When I do shameful things, I *want* to feel

> After repentance and forgiveness, I accept the gospel truth that there is now no condemnation for those who are in Christ Jesus.

shame because that's part of the process of change. After repentance and forgiveness, I accept the gospel truth that there is now no condemnation for those who are in Christ Jesus. Walking in grace, however, doesn't mean I shouldn't feel shame when I act shamefully; it means that after admitting my shame, I can be released from the guilt of my actions, encouraged by God's acceptance and love, and rest in His promised help and empowerment so that I can act in a less shameful way in the future.

Living in shame leads to all kinds of psychological ills and destruction; *passing through* shame can lead us to God, spiritual health, and even psychological balance. I don't want to grow up "feeling no shame" if that means I can act in a deplorable manner and just accept it as part of who I am.

If you're ashamed of how you've been living, embrace God's conviction, repent of your past lifestyle, receive God's forgiveness, rest in His acceptance, *but then* let the bitterness of your previous shame spur you toward a new life, knowing that you never want to taste that shame again. In other words, don't run from shame, run from the behavior that leads to shame.

Wicked behavior rightly brings shame and disgrace (Prov. 13:5). Paul says we should live in such a way that we have no need to be ashamed: "Do your best to present yourself to God as one approved, a worker who does not need to be ashamed" (2 Tim. 2:15). Paul's desire *not* to be ashamed is clear motivation for him to live a courageous life in Christ (Phil. 1:20). The apostle John likewise used the desire to not be ashamed as motivation for continued life in Christ: "And now, dear children, continue in him, so that when he appears we may be confident and unashamed before him at his coming" (1 John 2:28). John is keeping the fear of future shame alive to amend his present character.

Whenever shame is rejected, it's solely because we should not be ashamed of the gospel (Rom. 1:16) or our Lord (2 Tim. 1:8). The Bible doesn't reject shame as a response to immoral behavior, or call shame illegitimate when it's the result of cowardice and the rejection of our need to be active ministers of the gospel. On the contrary, shame is a legitimate, appropriate response to immoral, obnoxious, selfish behavior. Rather than run from it, we should allow it to motivate us toward godliness.

In this sense, shame is a God-created, God-designed emotional response intended to keep us from sliding even further away from His will when we act in an abominable, or even just an inappropriate way. It's a "check"—sort of like those truck ramps placed on the downhill side of mountain highways. When we're morally running out of control, and our normal conscience brakes aren't working, shame is God's gift to make us think twice: *Do I really want to live this way?*

Shame as a response to poor living isn't the problem; it's part of the cure. It's God's intention to point us back to Him.

So, if you've been experiencing shame in any part of your life, Jordan Easley invites you to accept the gospel truth that God's response to shame isn't just forgiveness—it includes *transformation.* The second-century bishop Irenaeus wrote, "The glory of God is man fully alive." If you've felt partially alive, trying to hide your shame rather than

> If you've felt partially alive, trying to hide your shame rather than seek transformation, welcome to the book you are about to read.

seek transformation, welcome to the book you are about to read. Read it slowly, thoughtfully, and prayerfully. Let God lead you to a new place beyond forgiveness—a place called transformation.

Gary Thomas

Best-selling author of *Pure Pleasure* and *Sacred Marriage*

Introduction

Do you know anybody who is desperate for life change? A spouse, a coworker, a friend, or . . . maybe you? It's likely that as you are reading this introduction, you are asking whether this book is going to work or not. You've been here before, wanting to make a change that will . . . well . . . change your life.

Maybe you've failed so many times that you've about given up hope. Or have you felt as though you were the only one struggling with change? You're definitely not when you consider this list of "how to" phrases I just searched for on Google:

- How to lose weight before my wedding: 19,600 results
- How to join Alcoholics Anonymous: 55,900 results
- How to stop biting my fingernails: 188,000 results
- How to quit smoking: 884,000 results

- How to keep New Year's resolutions: 1,030,000 results
- How to change my life: 5,740,000 results

You'd think that with all this information on the Internet—not to mention decades' (if not centuries') worth of self-help books—this industry would be shrinking instead of still growing. But most people are looking for their solutions in all the wrong places—especially when it comes to authentic life change.

What you'll discover throughout the pages of this book is—no matter how difficult it may be—true change is possible in your life! You're about to begin a journey in discovering what that looks like.

As we walk through the book of Mark, you will be introduced to several people who had unique stories and backgrounds. But one thing they all had in common was a desire for change: A leper whose need, hope, and faith brought him to Jesus. A paralytic who needed to change his environment first. A woman who lived twelve years in total isolation—no family, no friends, no touch, and no hope for change. A boy who had to fight against the change fighter—Satan—before he could experience the change factor.

As we peek into their lives, as well as others, there's a good chance God will reveal something about your own life and show you exactly how change can happen to you as well.

Life Change

Why we want it, need it, and why it's so hard to experience

Here's a little quiz for you (circle your answer, either physically or mentally):

1. Is there something in your life that needs to change? YES / NO
2. Can you change it? YES / NO
3. If it were a matter of life or death, could you change then? YES / NO

A wife says to her husband, "If you don't change, I'm leaving."

A doctor says to his patient, "If you don't change, you're going to die."

A financial planner says to his client, "If you don't change, you're going to lose everything."

A warden says to an inmate being released, "If you don't change, you're going to be back here soon."

Would you change anything in your life? Think for a second. What would it be? How would you do it and how would you make it last?

When it comes to change, the facts I've discovered about life change are discouraging. There was a new statistic released from the medical field recently. It stated that only one out of every ten people could change, even in a crisis environment. In a recent study of patients who have undergone major heart surgeries, researchers have found that two years after the surgery, ninety percent of those patients had not changed their lifestyle and found themselves in the very same health condition they were before surgery.

These are startling statistics when you think about it. They mean that the chance for change depends a lot on luck and circumstances beyond our control. When it comes to change happening in your life, the odds are stacked against you. Change sounds easy. It sounds doable. It sounds like it shouldn't be that great of a challenge, but when it comes to creating a lasting change in your life—real, authentic change—it's much easier said than done.

Merriam-Webster's dictionary defines *change* as to make or become different and to become different or replace with another. We all feel the need at times to become different in some way. Change is rooted in who we are as humans. In order to grow and develop in life, change is inevitable. Just Google "change theory" or "human development" and you'll get eyestrain reading the hundreds of articles and research papers on the many theories about change. Psychologists have some major theories associated with the process and complications of change for humans that span from ecological explanations to biological and social reasons. One thing that is clear from all the psychological research: the desire and need for change is felt by everyone and is an absolute necessity to being healthy and growing over time.

Whether we realize it or not, we've changed probably thousands of times over the span of our lives. In addition to the psychological, social, and biological reasons for wanting to change there are some spiritual reasons too. The Bible begins with the story of how everything in the beginning was perfect and then things fell

> Whether we realize it or not, we've changed probably thousands of times over the span of our lives.

5

apart. Suddenly, what was all right became in need of repair. From that moment in the garden, we have needed, wanted, and sought after some kind of change in our lives, even if we didn't know what those changes were. The apostle Paul wrote to the Christian groups living in Rome as early as the year 56, saying that because all of creation fell—the earth, the animals, and especially humans—they desperately want, are looking for, and expecting change.

Because of this, not all of our desires for change are obvious. Some of them are deeply hidden and can only be seen in the things that we do every day, like the things we buy or what we watch on television. We buy products and services. We are persuaded by countless commercials. And we watch hours of makeover and renovation television programs every single week. Companies around the world make billions of dollars selling everything from flake-free hair gel to knee-high argyle socks with the promise that they will make us feel better, make us look better, or just simply change our lives for the better.

In the mid- to late-1800s a Scottish gent named Samuel Smiles started a revolution we now call the self-help book industry. His book, simply titled *Self-Help*, sold more copies than Darwin's *On the Origin of Species*, to the tune of a quarter million books during his lifetime, which today would be the equivalent of a *New York Times* best seller. Smiles is cited with writing the famous maxim that many mistakenly attribute to the Bible: "Heaven helps those who help themselves." This self-help revolution that Smiles started has turned into a $10-billion business in the United States alone. As staggering as that figure sounds, it doesn't even include other book markets around the world. In the United Kingdom, self-help books have reportedly sold the equivalent of $100 million in just a five-year period. That is approximately one million self-help books sold per year.

Every year we set goals for our lives. We make promises to ourselves and to our loved ones, and we call these promises "New Year's resolutions." And the sad reality is that by the end of that year, we end up setting

> The sad reality is that by the end of that year, we end up setting many of the same goals we did twelve months earlier, hoping that our luck will change or we will magically become more disciplined.

many of the same goals we did twelve months earlier, hoping that our luck will change or we will magically become more disciplined and finally achieve the life change we've sought so many times before. The statistics are pretty staggering when it comes to the resolutions we make. Surveys suggest that most people don't even keep their New Year's resolutions past the first few weeks of the new year. Our spending of time and money on everything from creating feng shui in our homes and offices to relieving stress through yoga tells us that we are willing to go anywhere, consider anything, and do whatever it takes to get real, lasting change in our lives.

In case you're feeling extra-unspiritual because you can count on two hands (or more) the number of self-help books you've read or how many times you've set and reset New Year's resolutions, rest assured you're not alone. Here are some examples from the Bible of men and women who also struggled with this topic of change:

- Paul said that he did the things he didn't want to do and called himself a wretch and desperately asked for change.
- Jacob ran away from everyone, ashamed at the reputation that he gained himself as a liar and a thief. He desperately wanted to be changed.
- Adam and Eve hid from God and wondered what would happen to them.
- Joseph kept ending up in bad situations, time and time again.
- David proclaimed numerous times that he was helpless and doomed to be a "bad guy."
- Sarah laughed when God Himself promised her the unimaginable.

- Solomon wrote a whole book about how he had a bad attitude, lived a wasteful life, and finally realized when he grew older that he was still unable to do anything about it.
- Jeremiah desperately wanted to say all the crazy things that God told him to say but was too afraid of everyone and wished that he wasn't such a coward.
- Ruth, David's grandmother (and, thus, Jesus' ancestor), seduced a man to get him to like her.
- Peter, one of Jesus' twelve disciples, was a racist who didn't want to share the gospel of Jesus with people who weren't the same race as him, even though God told him that he needed to change his mind.

I mentioned Paul in that list of people in the Bible who needed change. Paul is a poster child for needing some dramatic changes. He could have been considered a Middle Eastern terrorist before becoming an apostle. He notoriously got permission from the religious leaders to kill the infidels, Christians. Once his life was transformed, Paul was not just an average Christian. He traveled the world and was imprisoned for telling others about Jesus. He weighed the pros and cons of staying on the earth or going to be in heaven with God. Even in this, Paul confessed how much he wanted to change the person he was in some other areas of his life. Paul was probably the guy written about as undergoing the most changes in his life in the New Testament. He began as a murderer of Christians, a religious zealot, and a Jewish terrorist, but became a church-starting, grace-loving peacemaker. Paul began as an arrogant proclaimer of the gospel and yet transformed into being a confident example of the gospel. His many insecurities, frailties, and challenges were basic human failings, but God turned those around and he eventually lived a changed life.

If we look around the world at the lives we lead today, and even of those in the Bible, we see life narrate the story of change. We know what we want, but why do we have so much trouble grasping it? Scripture not only points out those who wanted change but also promises that we'll find it rooted in what God wants to do in our lives. What is also clear in these examples is that change comes with its own set of challenges. However we want to slice it, we want change—no, we need change—and we must pursue it wholeheartedly.

> Scripture not only points out those who wanted change but also promises that we'll find it rooted in what God wants to do in our lives.

Whether it's a habit we want to kick or our entire lifestyle that needs an overhaul, change is often elusive or, at best, difficult to maintain. So why is it so hard, and what stands in our way? Not surprisingly, there has been an enormous amount of research done on the subject, and there are many reasons ranging from psychological to biological.

According to the creation account in Scripture, everything started out in a perpetual state of perfection. Then the devil stepped in and planted that doubt—"surely you won't die"—and the choice was made to disobey God. This choice declared that Adam and Eve wanted something other than God's perfect plan for them. They thought they knew better. Sounds familiar doesn't it? We make the similar choice on a daily basis. But as a result of the initial rebellion in the garden, Scripture says in the book of Genesis that when God took some things away, their "eyes became opened" and they knew they were naked.

Through these tragic series of events, humans became aware that we are missing something . . . and we've been looking for that something ever since. Now add to the story of the fall of man the mountain of scientific research about how we think, why we act the way we do, and what makes change so difficult and it begins to all add up. What the scientists have described for us is what happened to our hearts and minds after the fall. As a result of Satan's lies—which we still believe today—I believe there are four major challenges that prevent change.

Challenges That Prevent Change

1. Habits

Have you ever wondered why you're consistently a little short or behind on the electric bill when you make enough money? Or perhaps why you're always a few minutes late to work when there's no traffic? Could some unseen habit be what is holding you back from a life-changing promotion, getting out of debt, overcoming an illness, or transforming your marriage? Are your habits parading behind the scenes and causing you trouble? What we repeatedly and consistently do is one of the major challenges resisting our attempts at change.

Our habits—for better or worse—become who we are. Usually our habits happen even without us being aware. Habits, simply put, are those things we do so regularly that they become almost second nature. Habits turn us into robots, and any attempt to change our hardwiring is met with intense resistance. Are you a nail biter? A procrastinator? An overeater? Do you overspend? All of these are common habits that people perform on a daily basis without hardly being aware of them. These are easy to miss when we look at our life because they don't seem to be very problematic when we look at them as isolated moments in our days. Of course, there are some other habits that are obviously more damaging, like drug and alcohol abuse, lying, or stealing.

Habits form in our minds when we perform a particular action repeatedly in a specific context, such as a place or situation. Any behavior we practice with some consistency can become a habit and every habit is difficult to break. Yet, there's another hidden danger to habits that stand in our way. Habits can be the mischievous catalysts of problems in our life; they train us to act without thinking. And when our brains are programmed in such a way that our actions control us, it's difficult to free ourselves up to change.

2. Anxiety

You know anxiety. We've all felt it. Think back to your first job interview. How did you feel before you sat down to talk about how well qualified you were to flip burgers? Do you remember how you felt going on your first date? Or when you were about to get married? Or what about how you feel when you walk into a room filled with a bunch of strangers? In situations such as these, do you shut down? Get that deer-in-the-headlights look? Do you have trouble even forming proper sentences? Most people would describe these moments as very anxious experiences.

While we all handle these things differently, we all do experience some form of anxiety from time to time. When it comes to having to change something, the feeling of anxiety sets in when we feel that change is either impossible or simply too much for us to do on our own. By far, anxiety is the biggest (and perhaps the most powerful) challenge we face when trying to make significant changes in our lives.

Anxiety makes our hearts beat faster, our blood pump rapidly, collapses decision-making, and stops us from taking any kind of positive action. It is the most powerful reason change doesn't happen in our lives. Nothing can heighten anxiety more than when considering making some change in our lives no matter how big or small those changes might be.

Over the course of doing ministry, I've met people with pretty remarkable stories and have witnessed some amazing stories of life transformation. One of those people was a drug addict. When he reached the lowest point in his life, everyone thought he was either going to end up dead or in prison. His parents helped him get into a rehab program in a different city. When I talked to him while he was in rehab, he was making some progress. He said that he was thankful for the rehab community that he was a part of because they kept reminding him that he was an addict and that he could be drawn back to drugs at any time. Yet, he also stated that every day is a struggle because he feels overwhelmed by all the steps, all the meetings, and the constant checking up that has to happen to make sure he doesn't slip into drug use again. He confided in me that it was too much and wondered whether his life was going to be like that forever. Eventually the anxiety got the best of him and he went to get some relief in his old friend and overdosed.

My friend didn't fear the future of being a drug addict. That's not what kept him from change. What kept him from change was the feeling that he had to take on the whole system as it was described to him—to not succumb to drug abuse again—for the rest of his life. He was right. He only had part of the solution for real, lasting change. What he needed was help that was bigger than him.

The reality is that we all face that kind of anxiety. It's different from fear, doctors say. They instead describe it as an intimidation by our perception of what we are about to face. Some researchers call anxiety or worry our secret agenda.

> Some researchers call anxiety or worry our secret agenda. No matter how you look at it, there are agendas working against our goal for life change.

No matter how you look at it, there are agendas working against our goal for life change. That's why Jesus told His followers not to worry about anything. He didn't just give them the command to not worry. He explained that worrying about tomorrow or today, or truly about anything, wouldn't change the situation. He said, basically, "You're not in charge. So you don't need to worry about anything. You can't make your life better. You can't make your life anything, really." (See Luke 12:22–26.)

3. Beliefs

I walked into a friend's house one day and saw one of the weirdest things. His four-year-old son was crawling around on the floor on all fours and snarling. I looked at my friend in disbelief and said, "What is he doing?" He said, "He thinks he's a dog." I think anyone would agree that what you believe makes a difference. Our beliefs shape us. They determine what we want, how we think, and ultimately how we behave. Change is made even more difficult because of our beliefs. In fact, some of the other challenges to life change are tied to what we believe. The habits we develop, such as how we spend our money or how we celebrate or how we organize our time, are directly related to what we believe about certain things and about ourselves.

What we believe about God either helps us or hinders us when it comes to life change. One thing we'll discover is that prayer leads to change. But do we believe that God can hear and answer our prayers? Are there things, even in private, we feel a little embarrassed to ask God to do or give?

One of my pastor friends told a story about a woman in his congregation who didn't think that God could take more than one request at a time. He patiently, and lovingly, explained to her that if that were true then it would be impossible for God to answer any prayers because there were people all over the world praying all at once at any given time. She realized that it would make more sense that God is big enough to hear and answer multiple requests at the same time. Imagine how anxious she must have been about prayer.

We need to have the right kinds of beliefs when it comes to who God is and what God does. We also need to believe the right things about ourselves. Sometimes we overestimate our own capacity to make lasting changes. This goes back to our New Year's resolutions. For whatever reason, every year on January 1 we think we are suddenly capable of doing the impossible, just because the date changed on the calendar. We've given ourselves too much credit!

On the other hand, we sometimes fail to believe in ourselves altogether. I remember meeting a man who believed that God could never forgive him for the murder that he committed when he was young. I told him the story of Paul and how Paul was a mass murderer who killed people just because they were different from him. After talking with the man, I discovered it wasn't that he didn't believe God was big enough to forgive him—he was sure that if the same opportunity presented itself, he would probably do it again. He knew he hadn't changed. This man knew that

God was smart enough and big enough, but he thought that he was just simply too bad. What we believe can determine the direction and outcome of our lives. When it comes to life change, belief is the fuel that drives us toward either success or failure. It all depends on what we believe.

4. Competing Commitments

This is a new one in the science that looks at life change. It comes from the area called organizational psychology. In a study commissioned by Harvard, psychologists discovered why we resist change even when we know the change will be better for us. They call this a competing commitment. It's our innate immunity to change. Competing commitment simply means that we have a prior and much deeper commitment to something else. Whatever our competing commitment is, it will either interfere with (at best), or contradict (at worst), whatever our life change goal may be. The researchers called this "shoveling against the tide."

In the Bible we read the story of a rich young ruler who came to Jesus with a question: "Good teacher, what must I do to inherit eternal life?" Jesus answered by posing this thought-provoking question (actually, He offered a quick Q&A): "Why do you call me good? No one is good—except God alone." (See Mark 10:17–31 for the entire story.) Jesus was really doing two things in this response. First, Jesus asked him the question because the man assumed you had to be "good" to inherit eternal life. Second, since the man had called Jesus good, Jesus established His authority. Jesus was saying, "Yes. I am good, and since God is also the only one good, then by your own words I am God."

Jesus goes on to walk him through the commandments, finally telling him, "Go, sell everything you have, give the money to the poor, and then come follow me." The Bible says that this guy walked away sad, because he was very rich and wasn't willing to give up anything. What Jesus did was show the man that he broke the first commandment and, therefore, it was impossible for him to be "good." Jesus had asked just the right questions to make the man realize his competing commitment. Jesus showed him that he was more committed to himself and his money than he was to God. The kind of change he was looking for was staring him in the face, but when the solution was handed to him, he went in the opposite direction.

We all have competing commitments in our lives. The overwhelming commitment to ourselves builds a wall of resistance to the humility that change requires. It is far easier to dance in the mask of strength than it is to parade in the nakedness of desperation. What are the competing commitments in your life that keep you away from experiencing a change? Here's a better question for you: What would make

> What would make you uncomfortable in adopting the kind of change you want? Answer that and you have just discovered your competing commitment.

you uncomfortable in adopting the kind of change you want? Answer that and you have just discovered your competing commitment.

We Are Powerless

These startling discoveries show us that when it comes to change, we are virtually powerless. Although they don't eliminate the chance for change, they do make it look impossible. When it comes to making lasting change in your life, the odds are stacked against you. On the surface, even when considering these insights, making lasting changes in life shouldn't be such a great challenge—especially with a little organization, some motivation, and some support. Yet, what these studies and findings reveal is that even with the right motivation and in the most supporting circumstances, creating change in your life is too big to handle alone. The desire for change is a part of who we are, and yet, the resistance to change is a hurdle all of us have to jump over at one point or another.

From the Beginning

To understand this idea of being powerless to change, it is important to go back to the beginning. Not the beginning of this book, but to the beginning of human history. We touched on it a bit earlier in this chapter, but I think a full retelling of the story is important to fully appreciate how what's described in the Bible as the "fall" significantly affected all of life. Genesis tells the story this way (in my words): "In the beginning God created the heavens and the earth . . . and God saw that it was good . . . and God said don't . . . then they did . . . then something happened . . . and God said now how are you going to fix this?"

So God created the world in a condition that He described as "good." So, if you're like me, you're probably wondering, how could a God who is big and powerful ever make anything "good" that somehow turns "bad"?

Another way to look at this is that God created everything perfect. Perfect complicates the picture even more, doesn't it? People were created perfectly . . . and even now, we're still perfect when it comes to how God intended for us to operate. If you've ever designed, planned, or imagined anything and it came out just the way you had envisioned, you would say it turned out "perfect!" That's what happened to us.

Part of that perfect creation of human operation was choice. Humans are designed to make choices. As evidence, right now you're considering making the choice to believe this or not, to keep reading or to put down the book and turn on the television or do something else. Choice is hardwired in us. It comes with the package. God gave us choice. God gave us the choice to choose Him or to choose ourselves. God made us with choice so that our love and our choices would be real and not automatic or programmed.

According to Genesis, Adam and Eve chose themselves and, subsequently, everyone who followed them did the same. That, too, became ingrained in us. It isn't part of the original programming, but it became a habit that was taught and passed down throughout the generations. Yes, even you were taught it, whether you realize it or not. Let's do a quick checkup. What was your first thought this morning? If it wasn't God, there's your proof.

What Adam and Eve did was the equivalent of a toaster deciding to take its plug out of the wall, or a dog grabbing the leash and walking himself. When we choose to go our own way, we become disconnected from God. This only gets worse the further disconnected we get from the original Source. Ever played the "telephone game" or some variation of it? It's where someone whispers a phrase to the person next to him and that person whispers it to the next. You get the point. By the time it gets to the last person, they've got the message completely wrong. Well, imagine the telephone game multiplied a thousand times. Along the way in human history, the original message is not only distorted, no one even knows that there was an original message. That's where we are today: corrupted, misinformed, misguided, and unable to choose correctly because we're no longer connected to the Source of the reason our hearts beat.

God promised that when we choose ourselves, like a toaster not plugged in, we would die. God was saying that we would be useless. Not only that, but we physically die as well. Ever get the feeling we're supposed to live a long time? Do we ever feel frustrated about life or anxious about the time? It's because we know it's running out and somehow feel that it shouldn't. Or perhaps it's because we know that time for us shouldn't run out. Since that day we've wanted to know our purpose and had within us this innate sense of wanting to be connected to something or Someone greater than ourselves. We look for it in companionship, in work, in making things, but because we don't really know the best way to do this, we end up making mistakes, errors, and complete fumbles.

From the time we were children, we either thought that life would last forever or we never thought about it at all. Then things got complicated. We grew older, our parents gave us rules, then we became parents, gave rules to our little ones . . . and as the clock ticks, we grow more and more anxious. This anxiety, as pointed out earlier, completely paralyzes our ability to make the right choices—even though we want to do so immediately—because we are so overwhelmed by all we want to do in such a relatively short time. As a result, our misinformed choices force us to seek a change of direction.

Of course, not all of the things in our life come from our own individual choices, but everything is an indirect result of one single choice long ago—the moment Adam and Eve chose pleasure over God's instructions by eating the forbidden fruit. Scripture says that their eyes became opened; they knew they were naked, hid themselves, and looked for some way to change their condition. This is where the desire for change began. The Bible records that one of the first consequences to come about from the fall was that the things we would normally want to do as a part of our nature would become very difficult and seem like a waste of time.

> One of the first consequences to come about from the fall was that the things we would normally want to do as a part of our nature would become very difficult and seem like a waste of time.

One of the most obvious examples we have today that all human beings want to be changed is seen in the number of religions there are in the world. All of the religions have some system designed to change us, to make us a "better person." They promise us fulfillment, joy, peace, and an escape from the trivialities of life. All of our human history and all of the institutions we set up (not just religions) aim to do this. Take, for instance, all the businesses, products, and services available to help us change ourselves. Advertising agencies help companies make billions of dollars selling these things to us with the promise of making our lives better. Yet, no matter what we wear or where we go, we remain unchanged on the inside and have this nagging reminder deep down that we still don't know authentic life change.

Connectedness for Change

The only hope we have for real life change is found in getting and staying connected with God. If our disconnectedness makes us need and want change, then our connectedness is the only way to solve it. The Bible tells the story of God wanting to give us a new hope, a new way to think, and ultimately a new way to live. God has made this goal His pet project. The Bible refers to God as the God of hope, or the source of hope. *Hope* can be defined as a confident expectation. What that means is that we can be sure that whatever God promises to do He will do, or that whatever He promises to give He will give. We can be sure because it is almighty God who promises it. In Psalm 33:17 it says, "A horse is a vain hope for deliverance; despite all its great strength it cannot save." This means that all the self-help books in the world and all the self-improvement products in the world *combined* can't change our lives. They might help us get from point A to B, earn a promotion at work, lose a few pounds, or get more organized, but they won't give us victory in the end. In other words, they won't last.

Being reconnected with God gives us hope and the power to change. Without connection to God, we have no hope. It says in Ephesians 2:12 to "remember that at that time you were separate from Christ, excluded from citizenship in Israel and foreigners to the covenants of promise, without hope and without God in the world." God wants to be connected with us because He also wants to change the way we think. When we consider everything we discussed so far, our minds have a lot to do with our problems. How we think is one of the major challenges that stands in the way of change.

If I were to come to you one day and offer you a million dollars (not that I have it) with no conditions, would you take it? If your answer is yes, what would you do with it? Now that you're back to reading after daydreaming about this, you probably have a list in your mind of all the dramatic changes you'd make in your life as a result of that large sum of money. Even if you said you would use some of it to help the poor, feed the hungry, or bless your church, the fact is you listed some things you would buy too. What are those things? Do they glorify God? Here's the key question: Did you even consider whether or not God would want those new things in your life? The fact is, we don't think the way God wants us to think. And if you're a Christian, the answers you gave probably weren't different from those given by people who are not connected to God. God has to change the way we think.

When God told Abraham that he was going to give him and his wife, Sarah, a new child when they were more than eighty years old, Abraham probably showed God the doctor's report. The Bible says that Sarah laughed. What they needed to undergo was a radical transformation in the way that both Sarah and Abraham thought. They needed to understand that God could do anything. So, over the course of the years following that particular promise, they reconnected with God, and God changed their minds. He wants to do the same with all of us. What it says in Romans 12:2 is pretty interesting: "Do not conform any longer to the pattern of this world, but be transformed by the renewing of your mind. Then you will be able to test and approve what God's will is—his good, pleasing and perfect will." It says that when we let God change our minds, He'll change our life, too, because we will know what He wants us to do. Do you see the very simple equation for life change that God laid out for us? It goes like this: reconnect with God and He will inspire hope in you that will change your mind and ultimately your life.

Change Is Possible

Regardless of how difficult it seems or how long you've been facing whatever your particular challenge may be, Jesus gives these comforting words to us: "With God all things are possible" (Matt. 19:26). So no matter how you slice it, change is available when God is the one orchestrating the change. We have a mountain of psychological, emotional, and spiritual reasons to believe that change is impossible, but the Bible says it truly is possible with God. As you continue reading this book, you'll meet individuals from the book of Mark who discovered that a connection to God through Jesus brings a solid hope for change. And such incredible, lasting, life change can happen in your life too.

> Regardless of how difficult it seems or how long you've been facing whatever your particular challenge may be, Jesus gives these comforting words to us: "With God all things are possible" (Matt. 19:26).

CHAPTER 2

A Life in Need of Healing

What happens when you mix desperation with faith in the healer?

You say you want to change. Then ask yourself this question: *When was the last time I was desperate for Jesus?* And the reason that question is so important at the beginning of this journey is because when you're desperate, it changes everything! You may be surprised to find that desperation is actually the opposite of hope. Desperation, which you may need more than you realize, is the starting point to the spiritual operation God wants to perform so you can have a new life.

We begin our journey toward change with the story of a man who, because of his skin condition of leprosy, was keenly aware of his need for Jesus. When I first read the story of the leper in Mark 1:40–45, what really stood out about this man was the fact that he was on his knees begging Jesus to change him. This man was *desperate*!

Not long ago, I decided to take a few youth pastors out to one of my favorite lunch spots. This particular restaurant is famous for its steak fajitas, so naturally I ordered a fajita platter for the entire table. The guys were excited, not only because of the homemade tortillas and bottomless chips and queso . . . but they were excited because it was *free*. After about fifteen minutes, the platter arrived, and it looked great. It was full to the brim with sizzling steak and grilled vegetables. Everyone began filling their plates with food simultaneously.

I noticed Ryan putting one of the red peppers on his plate. I was under the impression that the red and orange peppers were there for decoration. I had never thought about eating one, so I asked him if he had ever tried one. He quickly responded, "No," yet he didn't seem concerned about it at all. At that point, the other guys around the table began looking at one another because they knew what was about to happen as soon as he bit into that pepper.

As Ryan took that first bite, one of the other guys removed his water glass from the table. Everyone else followed suit and removed their water from the table as well. So now Ryan was left without anything to drink as he bit into the pepper. But it didn't look like he was going to need a drink. He didn't flinch, not even a little bit . . . for about ten seconds . . . and then his face turned a shade of red I've never seen before. His eyes were immediately bloodshot, and tears began streaming down his cheeks.

The other guys around the table were laughing so hard that they forgot to put the water back on the table. He had to get something to drink! So without any hesitation or reservation, he stood to his feet and began running around the restaurant screaming.

He finally located a pitcher of water on another table, which was occupied by an older couple enjoying their lunch. Without asking, he grabbed the pitcher, held it up to his face, and chugged the water until it was completely empty. He was desperate, and his desperation drove him to grab that pitcher of water from someone else's table—something he would never have done under normal circumstances. But this was not a normal situation. When you're desperate, everything changes.

The leper in this Bible story had experienced a level of desperation that far exceeded what my friend went through in the restaurant that day. Eating a hot pepper couldn't begin to bring about the pain a leper feels. Doctor Luke tells us in his account that this man was "full of leprosy" (5:12 NKJV), which would be the equivalent of a cancer patient today being identified as "stage 4."

This man's body was overcome by leprosy, and it was a vicious disease that attacked the body. If diagnosed with it, you were legally forbidden to have any contact with the outside world. According to Leviticus 13:45–46:

> The person with such an infectious disease
> must wear torn clothes, let his hair be unkempt,
> cover the lower part of his face and cry out,
> "Unclean! Unclean!" As long as he has the
> infection he remains unclean. He must live
> alone; he must live outside the camp.

The law was clear. If you had leprosy and found yourself near other people, you were legally required to scream, "Unclean! Unclean!" and then turn and run in the opposite direction.

Here is this desperate guy who was tired of living this way. He was tired of being an outcast. He was tired of the sores and the shame and the embarrassment, and his desperate need brought him to Jesus. But he didn't come to Jesus just to get rid of something (his disease). No, hope brought him to Jesus as well.

Hopelessness can lead to *despair*. It is easy to think that whatever is broken in our lives cannot be fixed, or that we cannot be freed from whatever has held us captive. This despair sets in when we realize how powerless and ill equipped we are to change anything and anyone, especially our self. The feelings of being overwhelmed, outraged, guilty, and ashamed are the result of the anguish we experience when there is a lack of desperation in our lives. We become defeated because we're unable to even emotionally pull ourselves together to begin charting a course to healing.

> The difference in this particular leper's life was his focus. His eyes were not primarily focused on his own inability but were set on the ability and power of Jesus.

With all that being true, this leper may have been ill and a social outcast, yet he was not short-limbed by his condition in reaching for hope. The difference in this particular leper's life was his focus. His eyes were not primarily focused on his own inability but were set on the ability and power of Jesus. He was not the only leper, he was one among many, perhaps thousands in a community in which he lived. But he had reached the point where he told himself, and maybe even others, that he had had enough. He would rather be stoned to death for violating the law than spend another day having his hopes, dreams, and desires aborted because of an unfortunate condition of his skin. It takes more than a need to experience change in your life. If change is going to happen, we have to have hope. Hope is something that allows us to move toward change. Hope is required for action.

We would have considered his situation hopeless. This is where his desperation sets in. There were no physicians, there were no treatments, there were no medicines or medical teams . . . yet, he had hope. For some reason, there was no doubt in his mind that Jesus had the power to heal his disease. This guy told Jesus, "If you are willing, you can make me clean" (Mark 1:40). Read that again: "If you are *willing* . . ." not "If you are able. . . ." He believed that Jesus could heal him. He had *hope*.

There was something greater than this man's need or hope at work that sent him on his knees begging. It was his faith. Some people would look at that and say, "How do you know he had faith? How do you know it wasn't just hope? Why do you think it was faith?"

Paul describes in Romans 4 how faith works—how it's born from desperation—and he gives the example of Abraham. Not only was Abraham the "father of many nations" but he was also called the "father of faith." Paul wrote, "Against all hope, Abraham in hope believed" (v. 18). What Paul was saying was that Abraham and Sarah's doctor report left Abraham feeling hopeless, but it was in this hope-lessness that Abraham looked toward God, whom He was convinced was able to do what he had hoped for even when the situation was, well, hopeless.

Hopelessness, very simply put, is despair. Paul wrote that when looking at the facts, Abraham was hopeless and in despair. We shrink into despair because of the size of the problem and the lack of alternatives. Yet unlike many people in despair, Abraham didn't run out of places to turn. He turned to God in that desperation, hoping that God would change the situation. He was certain God *could* change the situation, but his response, like that of the leper, was to ask if God would. That is faith. Desperation, when combined with a focus on God's ability, produces life-changing faith.

What Paul demonstrated through talking about Abraham was the genesis, or the birth, of faith. This is how faith is born and this is how faith works. It works from des-peration. Later, the book of Hebrews picks up on this and gives an even clearer and more succinct definition. It says, "faith is the substance of things hoped for, the evidence of things not seen" (11:1 NKJV). So faith is both substance and evidence. To put it another way, faith is the temporary stand-in for what we hope for and having faith shows that we are convinced that we have what we hope for.

So the recipe for genuine, life-altering faith is this:

- one part desperation,
- one part belief in the ability of God, and
- one part meeting God in the unseen and preparing for what you expect God to do.

Hebrews 11:6 says, "And without faith it is impossible to please God, because anyone who comes to him must believe that he exists and that he rewards those who earnestly seek him." This guy might have had the faith of a mustard seed, but just a little faith goes a long way with God.

This man, full of leprosy, was desperate, and it was his need, his hope, and his faith that brought him to Jesus. But notice, this man's circumstance didn't end with him being desperate. You see this idea of faith demonstrated in the fact that he didn't remain hopeless. He went from being desperate to being cleansed: "Filled with compassion, Jesus reached out his hand and touched the man. 'I am willing,' he said. 'Be clean!' Immediately the leprosy left him and he was cured" (Mark 1:41–42).

I love the phrase that says Jesus was "moved with compassion" (NKJV). The original translation of that phrase basically means "to be inwardly disturbed with compassion." Compassion is more than concern. It's love in action. Jesus looked at this desperate man, overcome with leprosy, and seeing his hope and faith, He was moved to cleanse him of the wretched disease that had plagued him for so long.

What would it be like to be a leper? Think about it—an outcast, someone who was shunned and not even considered human by most people. If we had leprosy, the majority of our body would be an open wound, and we would be seen as a disgusting waste of life to everyone around us. Nobody would come near us, much less touch us. That's what this man was dealing with up until Jesus, being moved with compassion, cleansed him.

Desperation is the feeling we get when we look at the circumstances or the situation and feel that there is no way that it could change. As a result, scientists say, when we become desperate we make rash choices that we wouldn't under normal circumstances. That description seems to fit what this leper experienced. He wasn't supposed to have contact with anyone. The only people he could touch were people who were obviously "unclean" like him. Yet, this leper was desperate, and in his desperation he looked up to Jesus. Up to this point, the mind of this leper was filled with thoughts of despair. He had thoughts just like we do—thoughts of anger, thoughts of sadness, thoughts of loneliness and strife. His thoughts in his past were plagued with thoughts of hopelessness, and then he met Jesus. Suddenly everything became possible and this hope changed everything. His thinking had been changed.

He was operating outside of the normal constraints of the society he lived. He sought Someone who he was convinced had the power to heal him. The leper exhibited incredible fearlessness in approaching Jesus. And the reason he didn't hesitate was because desperation destroys the concern for what other people think is acceptable. He was possessed by desperation and convinced that Jesus could heal. What consumed him was his desire to be changed, to the point that he had given little to no regard for the rules or etiquette in approaching this Holy Man.

And that's so essential because what he needed—as we all need—is a different way of thinking that leads us to the right course of action. God grants this new way of thinking to those who trust Him. The thoughts of unworthiness and uncleanness suddenly vanished from his mind. Why? Because God was responding to his genuine faith by changing his thinking so that he would no longer be controlled by the fear that kept him away. When your goal for life change meets the transformative power of God, those goals truly become possible.

When this man's thinking changed, he was left with a few important decisions to make. Was he going to sit on the sidelines forever and accept what seemed to be the inevitable, or was he willing to charge onto the field and chase life? These were the things that he was considering. He had a lifetime of experience to know how deeply incapable he was of changing anything. He couldn't even change his address. He was desperate because he had seen the life of other lepers with his own eyes, but he was full of faith because he had envisioned a prosperous future and believed change was possible. Talk was all over town about Jesus' ability to heal. He knew that Jesus was able, and the only question that remained unanswered was, "Will He?" The leper demonstrated the principle found in Romans 10:17 that "faith comes from hearing . . ." Jesus' ability to heal was famous. He heard it, but the decision that came down for him, and for us, is the decision to believe it and pursue it.

Have you considered how big God really is? He has demonstrated that He can bring a child from a barren womb. He has demonstrated that He can bring an immeasurable universe into existence with a whisper. He has demonstrated that He can make fingerprints differ in innumerable ways. He knows the number of hairs you have on your head,

> Have you considered how big God really is? He has demonstrated that He can bring a child from a barren womb. He has demonstrated that He can bring an immeasurable universe into existence with a whisper.

regardless of how easy that might be for some of us these days. He doesn't just know yours, He knows that for everyone. With an eye on the enormity of God and having the confidence that He is able to do more than we can think or imagine, picture what our lives would look like if we took a chance on God and pursued Him relentlessly and desperately today.

One of the most difficult things to alter is our thought patterns. Thought patterns are ways of thinking that we are strongly attached to. So much of our life is built on them and that's part of the reason why they are so difficult to break down or to change. Yet the new life in Christ is a picture of a complete change of who we are. Paul wrote in 2 Corinthians 5:17, "If anyone is in Christ, he is a new creation; the old has gone, the new has come!" He wrote about the subject of thinking differently in Romans 12:2 as well saying, "Do not conform any longer to the pattern of this world, but be transformed by the renewing of your mind. Then you will be able to test and approve what God's will is—his good, pleasing and perfect will."

If we want to experience this new life we have to have a new way of thinking. Jesus said, "You don't put new wine in old wine skins" (Mark 2:22, author paraphrased). When Jesus made this statement, He was making a reference that his audience understood. The reason you didn't put new wine in an old wine skin was because the new wine would expand during the fermentation process and the expansion would destroy both the wine and the wine skin. He was illustrating the fact that you can't mix your old religious thoughts and your old ritualistic ideas with a new faith in Jesus. He was showing his disciples that faith in Jesus requires a new way of thinking.

Albert Einstein, one of the great, visionary thinkers of the modern era said that it was insane to do the same thing over and over again and expect different results. There is absolutely no way to become a new person without allowing God to change our thinking. Remember, changed thinking means progress, and old, stale, thinking means insanity.

I have a friend who has struggled in the past with her appearance. As a result she has battled various eating disorders including anorexia, bulimia, and forced starvation. She talked about the horrors of facing herself in the mirror every morning before the start of her day. She saw her future. What she saw was the image of the hospital and the morgue. She didn't need binoculars to look distantly into her future because her eating disorders were currently raging out of control.

With the support of some friends and tuning her ears to the Healer, she heard the echoing calm of words that told her she was beautiful. Written on her mirror in lipstick are the words, "You are made in the image of God," and, "Every hair on your head is counted," and, "Let the meditation of my heart, and the words on my lips be acceptable to you Lord." This wasn't some positive confession that promises that if you only say the right words, like a spell out of the Harry Potter books, your life will change. No, this was a desperate attempt to adjust her heart receptors and refocus her eyes on the Maker and Shaper of life who put beauty in her own soul. She no longer looks into a mirror and is haunted by her reflection, but into one that reflects and shouts "beautiful" as if it were her name.

My friend was plagued with a dangerous disease that gave her no certain future. Yet, despite that grim outlook she approached the Designer of futures who moved her to reexamine her influences. God changed her thoughts and saved her life. That reminds me of something Guy Fawkes, a British terrorist from the 1600s who inspired the film *V for Vendetta,* said: "A desperate disease requires a dangerous remedy." He thought that things had gotten so bad in Great Britain that the only way to fix the ills of their government was to ignite enough gunpowder to collapse the government buildings along with its regal inhabitants.

He unfortunately didn't look to the King with cattle on a thousand hills. Only God can provide the "dangerous remedy." What he thought would be a prescription for national revolution turned out to be a poison for personal disaster. Fawkes was later tortured, tried, and disgustingly executed. Because he was convicted of high treason, which is criminal disloyalty to your own government, he was executed in a fashion they coded "halfway between heaven and earth, as unworthy of both."

Fawkes didn't have faith in God, and so his thinking only left him with human solutions, and evil ones at that. God could have given him the necessary thoughts for the kind of radical transformation that would have benefited everyone. He ultimately failed because he was applying old thinking to old problems wanting new results. If he would have asked the maker of governments, God would have given him new thoughts and made him a national hero of tremendous influence rather than allowing him to become publicly humiliated.

What hangs in the balance for all of us is a thriving, vibrant future full of the possibilities to lead full lives. That's the vision the leper had. For him the vision might have been as simple as being able to go into the marketplace and buy a loaf of bread. Can you imagine that? We take it for granted because it's part of our everyday routines, and it's actually something we complain about having to do. Pastor and author Erwin McManus writes in his book *Soul Cravings,* ". . . we thrive when we are optimistic about the future. It seems failure is no match for the person who believes in the future. When we see failure as personal, pervasive, or permanent, we become paralyzed."

As faith in God produces new ways of thinking, lack of faith keeps the old thoughts and leaves our lives without even the dust of hope for change. Real hope leads to a blindingly bright vision of the future that changes who we are to our very core.

One of my friends went through a rough time over the span of three years. Prior to that he was a guy full of faith and a strong Christian influence and testimony. But during those tough times his faith was shaken. He abused drugs and alcohol, and lost any hope for a changed life and became suicidal. After trusting Jesus again I knew he had hope for the future because I could hear it in his voice. He told me the story of how an old friend called him and said, "You sound different." When he asked how, the caller told him, "You don't sound as dejected." His life change didn't come overnight but when it came, everyone could see it.

This reminds me of when the famed actor Christopher Reeve (best known for his role as Superman) plummeted head first into a beam after having been catapulted from his horse. He ended up paralyzed. How strange that all of a sudden Reeve—the "Man of Steel" on the big screen—could no longer control his body. His accident had thrust him headfirst into the reality of life change. On the screen he melted metal with his eyes, caught bullets with his teeth, and treated steel planes as baseball bats. In his off-screen life, he seemed to embody illimitable energy in every aspect of his life. Reeve was an award-winning, competitive horse rider. One day he was harnessing the reins of his horse, appearing virtually unstoppable—in true Superman style—leaping boundlessly, and full of force. The next day he was relegated to the chains of immobility and pushed through life at the pace of others. Later he died from other complications caused by the accident. What we know all too well, demonstrated in this story, is that the change that alters the course of our lives can happen in an instant. This was the quality of change the leper sought when he decided to disregard convention and thrust himself at the feet of Jesus. This is the kind of change that is available to us.

There's a pretty good chance that your body isn't overcome with leprosy. You don't have open sores. You're probably not being shunned. However, you may be as desperate as the leper when it comes to your need for cleansing today. Where do you need change the most? Are there sins that haunt you? Is there one sin in particular that continually pops up in your life? Is there something that you fall victim to here and there that you know is wrong? You know you need to change. But your natural tendency is to try to change yourself.

We gossip to our friends and share stories that we know we shouldn't, and after we're finished we promise ourselves we won't do it again. We have pride in our hearts and we commit to overcoming the entitlement we live with each and every day. We make plans to become generous, but we can't because of our overwhelming greed that keeps us slave to our lenders (including college loans, car payments, mortgage, etc.). We promise to have peace, but we can't because of our constant worry. We say we're going to quit cursing or drinking or verbally abusing the ones we love. We want to believe we are strong enough to eliminate the lust of our eyes or the addiction to pornography that continues to grab hold

> We want to believe we're strong enough to change, but sooner or later we are forced to understand that we cannot change our lives.

of our hearts. We want to believe we're strong enough to change, but sooner or later we are forced to understand that we cannot change our lives.

You cannot change your life by yourself!

In the Bible, leprosy was a picture of sin. And just as leprosy separated the leper from society, sin separates a sinner from God. A person wasn't a leper because they had horrible ulcers and sores on their body. Their ulcers and sores were the result of the disease that they had within them. And just as leprosy began on the inside and worked its way to the outside where it could be detected, the sins in our hearts work their way to the outside where they can be detected as well. You're not a sinner because you sin—you sin because you are a sinner. And just as there was no cure for leprosy except by the power of God, there is no cure for sin except by Jesus' saving power. You cannot change yourself!

Notice the leper didn't have any question about whether Jesus could cleanse him—he just wasn't certain that Jesus would do it. And so it is with us today. We know that God is all-powerful and is able to cleanse us of our sins—but will He? And His answer is always the same: "I am willing; be cleansed" (Mark 1:41 NKJV).

Now did you notice He didn't say, "I am willing; be healed?" In fact, the leper didn't seek healing; he sought cleansing. "If you are willing, you can make me clean" (1:40 NKJV). Going back to the Leviticus 13 passage, we see that lepers were considered unclean and that leprosy was an emblem of sin. So when it came to the removal of leprosy, just as it is with sin today, cleansing is what's needed, not healing.

The One who was able to cleanse this man's sickness is able to cleanse your sin. Isaiah 1:18 says, "'Come now, and let us reason together,' says the Lord. 'Though your sins are like scarlet, they shall be as white as snow; though they are red as crimson, they shall be like wool.'" First John 1:9 says, "If we confess our sins, He is faithful and just to forgive us our sins and to cleanse us [not heal us] from all unrighteousness" (NKJV).

You may read that and say, "Okay, I get that, but can Jesus really change me?" Listen, not only is he able . . . He is *willing*! "I am willing; be cleansed." You see, Christ is the ultimate agent of change, and He wants more than anything for us to be desperate for Him and Him alone. For the leper, it was his need, his hope, and his faith that brought him to Jesus. For us, He desires the same.

So before you turn even one more page and continue this journey of discovering how real life change can become a reality for you, ask yourself these questions:

- Am I truly desperate for Jesus?
- Do I have a need for Him?
- Do I find hope in Him?
- Do I have faith in Him?

CHAPTER 3

How to Position Your Life for Change

What position does your life have to be in for real lasting change?

It was never a good thing when my dad called a family meeting. The summer after my third grade year, he called a meeting that would literally change the course of my life. He said the words every preacher's kid has heard at one point or another, "God has called us to another church and we are going to be moving soon."

Those words left me devastated! Apparently my parents didn't understand that I was pretty well established where we were. I had great friends, a school that I loved, and there was nothing inside of me that desired the kind of change that I was facing head-on. Needless to say, despite my fighting and bickering, my parents packed up our entire house, loaded up the car, and we looked at everything we knew as normal in the rearview mirror.

I never will forget the terror I felt later that summer as we prepared to begin the fall at a brand new school. Typically buying school supplies was fun, but this time it was different. My mind wasn't focused on what Trapper Keeper would be the coolest or what color my backpack was because I was too busy wondering how I would be able to make this life-altering adjustment.

On the first day of school, I woke up and made my way to the kitchen. My mom had breakfast on the table and our brand new backpacks in our chairs, filled with our new school supplies. As I opened the main zipper, I realized that she had actually put more than pencils, erasers, and a couple of packages of notebook paper in the backpack. There were also about twenty packs of gum. I asked my mom for an explanation and she told me that giving away gum might just help me make some new friends. She went on to show me how. She said, "When you get to the lunch room, look around at all the tables. When you see the table of boys that you think you want to be friends with, go up to them and ask them if they want a pack of gum."

Sounded like a decent plan, so when it came time for lunch, I did exactly what she said. I stood at the top of the stairs leading into the lunchroom and observed all the strangers as they sat eating their food. I looked at a table of kids that looked like scientists and thought . . . nope. There was a table of kids that looked like drug dealers and thought . . . not a good idea. In the back of the room was a table of kids dressed in all black and I'm pretty sure half of the boys were wearing eye makeup . . . not for me. Finally, I saw the table filled with kids that I wanted to join. These guys looked nice. They played sports and seemed to be respected by all the other students. It was obvious that these guys were the most popular guys in the room, and despite my initial hesitation, I approached them as instructed.

"My name is Jordan. I'm new. Uhhh . . . You guys want a pack of gum?" The response was unanimous and they all began reaching and fighting for the gum. What happened next was unexpected though. Even though there was an empty seat at the table, as I began to sit down, the ringleader of the guys said, "Sorry man, but you can't sit here." I walked away with my head down, but inside I was motivated to be a part of that circle.

As I evaluated what had happened, I began looking at myself and asking the question, "Why wasn't I accepted?" Once that question was asked, I began noticing that there were some major differences between me and these guys. I wore Nike tennis shoes and they all wore Reebok Pumps. I had a head full of hair and these guys had buzz cuts. I drank Coca-Cola and these guys drank Dr. Pepper. I wore off-brand clothes and these guys had the latest and the greatest. For the first time in my life, I realized that if I wanted to fit in to my surroundings, then I was going to have to change some things about myself, and change I did. Within weeks, I was walking like these guys, talking like these guys, and dressing like these guys. I looked the part, but even then, I still wasn't a part of their group.

I'll never forget the day my mom walked into the house after getting the mail and said, "Jordan, you got something." I opened the envelope and inside found an invitation to "the ringleader's" birthday party campout. It was official, I was in! I showed up at the party and it was just as I had expected. It was at his ranch; his parents were there, all the guys from the table were there, presents were being opened, and the cake was delicious. The party was perfect.

Then the parents went in the house and let us finish the party by ourselves. We pitched the tents, built a fire, and fished at his pond for a couple hours. But when the parents turned the house lights off, the party took a turn. The birthday boy pulled out one final present. This one was from his older brother and, for some reason, he was pretty excited about it. As he opened it, I realized why. There was a case of Bud Light, five *Playboy* magazines, and a carton of Marlboro cigarettes. There we were, eight elementary school-aged boys about to embark on a night we would never forget.

The beer began making the rounds and cigarette smoke filled the air. Guys were passing me things I had only heard about or seen in movies, and I was experiencing a battle like I had never experienced before. I remember filling my mouth with warm beer and feeling my gag reflex kick in. I remember the first puff of the cigarette and feeling like my insides were going to explode. I can still recall the thoughts that went through my head that night: *What in the world am I doing?*

"It's time to do something else!" The ringleader made it clear that he was ready to do something new and he told the rest of us to follow him. He made his way to the edge of his property. It was on a hill and overlooked a major interstate. Trucks were flying by at seventy miles per hour and he decided it would be fun to throw balls of clay at them as they passed. Everyone began making these balls out of the red clay on the side of the hill and then

> Someone noticed that I wasn't participating and the ringleader called me out. He said, "Hey Easley, are you with us or not?" He had no clue how powerful that question was.

they would take turns hurling them onto the road as trucks would pass. Apparently someone noticed that I wasn't participating and the ringleader called me out. He said, "Hey Easley, are you with us or not?" He had no clue how powerful that question was that day. It was a question I answered, not with my words, but with my actions. I picked up a rock, packed it with red clay, and prepared to throw it at the next vehicle. It didn't matter if it was a truck, a car, or a scooter, I was going to throw it as hard as I could.

Everyone watched as we saw the headlights coming from the distance. They got closer and closer, and we could finally hear the tires on the pavement and the roar of the engine. Someone screamed, "Throw it!" and I did. It was a perfect throw. It was the right distance. It had the right velocity. It was so perfect that the next sound we heard was the shattering of glass. Following that sound was the sound of screeching tires as the car did a one-eighty in the middle of the highway. The next sound was the other seven boys screaming, "Let's get out of here!" and "RUN!" But as we looked up at the car, we saw something we were not prepared for: red and blue lights. The lights were flickering, the siren came on, and the search light on the side of the car began picking us off as we ran through the woods. We ran, but it didn't matter how fast or where we went. It didn't change the fact that I had just hit the sheriff's deputy in the middle of the night with a clay-packed rock and nearly caused him to flip his squad car.

The officer made his way to the house and informed the parents of what had just happened. Some of the boys had to make their way to the station because they had previous offenses, but my consequence was much more severe. My dad was called.

After that night, I obviously had a lot of time to myself. It was one of those "You're grounded forever" seasons of my life, but as I reminisced on what happened, the reality of my actions really began to sink in.

There were questions I was trying to address as a preteen that most adults still struggle with today. Questions like: "Who am I?" "What is my purpose?" "How do I want other people to view me?" "Where am I valuable?" And the fact of the matter is that the places we go, the people we spend time with, and the positions we find ourselves in will determine a lot with regards to answering these questions. Our responses in these situations will dictate and determine the path we travel and the destination in which we arrive.

We need to ask ourselves who we want to be and what we want to do and where we want to go, because the answers to these questions reveal the true intent of our hearts. The early churches, right after Jesus ascended into heaven, had these same questions. They wondered what kind of lives they

> We need to ask ourselves who we want to be and what we want to do and where we want to go, because the answers to these questions reveal the true intent of our hearts.

should be living now that their eternal destinies had been changed. Paul basically told them that it was actually quite simple. He wrote to the churches in Rome at the time saying in Romans 12:2, "Do not be conformed to this world" (NKJV). The truth Paul was conveying was that our natural tendency is to change who we are in order to fit into our environment.

Your Surroundings

Your environment will determine your destination.

If you were to be honest, the reason why you may be one of the people reading this book is because an environment you were in or are currently in has led you to where you are now. There are countless stories of men and women, and boys and girls, who can retrace their steps to when their own lives took a turn for the worse. There are even more people who can tell us about the impossibility of climbing out of the hole that seems to only get deeper with each passing day.

The influences of our environments have the ability to alter our destiny. This is recorded in a powerful story in the Bible, found in the second chapter of Mark. It records the story of one occasion where Jesus had gone to a city named Capernaum. Because Jesus was so popular and was sought after by so many people, they needed an amphitheater to hold all of them, but all they had was a house. The Scripture says, "So many gathered that there was no room left, not even outside the door" (Mark 2:2).

Because of Jesus' popularity in His ability to heal, people would come from all over seeking healing, a message from God, or anything that would change their lives. Could you imagine the intensity of the moment? Imagine you lived fifty to a hundred miles away from the place that you hear a healer, with amazing powers, was going to be and you're not a skeptic. You're not skeptical because the pain you're experiencing is so excruciating that if a person told you a squirrel could heal, you would learn to climb a tree and catch squirrels with your bare hands all day, every day. That describes the desperation of Jesus' audience that day.

In the crowd, there was an odd group of men who themselves needed no healing but were carrying their friend who did. This friend was paralyzed and lying on a mat. They couldn't get to Jesus through any normal routes. But instead of going home, they looked for another way in. One of them spotted an opening in the roof. The room Jesus was in was so full—and probably the house too—they couldn't get to Him. What they did was uncommon, but really quite remarkable.

How crazy is that? Most people would just leave. Some would have left because of fear, scoffing, "I'm not going through the roof." Others would have been discouraged by the size of the crowd and would have gone away completely dejected. These men and the paralytic were noticeably different from everyone else. They were absolutely convinced, and were willing to do whatever it took to get their friend in a position that would at the very least expose him to Jesus.

They were so noticeably different that among all the people in the room begging for Jesus' attention, He noticed them. What Jesus noticed about this paralytic man was his faith. Here's what it says in verse 5: "When Jesus saw their faith, he said to the paralytic, 'Son, your sins are forgiven.'" I find it interesting that Jesus didn't just notice this about the paralytic man, because it says, "their faith." It was *their* faith that got Jesus' attention.

These friends of the paralytic weren't good friends, they were great friends. Their friendship was apparent, and that is demonstrated by their persistence and willingness to go on the journey with him and do whatever it took to see that their friend was healed. The course of his life and his future was changed because of one amazing event that took place due to the influence of faithful friends. These friends

had, maybe without even realizing it, influenced the direction of his life. Undoubtedly they were also changed by the
experience.

What the paralytic seemed to have been aware of is that
whom you surround yourself with has a bearing on the
direction in your life. He
must have known that. He
chose loyal, loving, persistent, and faithful friends
who had the same hope
and beliefs he did. He chose

> What the paralytic seemed
> to have been aware of is
> that whom you surround
> yourself with has a bearing
> on the direction in your life.

friends who were going in the direction that he wanted to
go. I'm sure that he had many alternatives and perhaps even
more friends. But what the story of this man's life suggests
to us is that these were his closest friends, his most trusted
friends, who shared his hopes, his values, his dreams, and his
goals in life.

As much as this principle works in the direction of positive life change, it can also work toward negative life change.
As much as our friends influence our direction for good, they
can also be an amazing—obvious or not-so-obvious—wall of
resistance to good in our lives. The bottom line of friendships is that our friends help shape and perfect our thinking. Anything can become perfected. Perfect just means it's

gotten to a level where it is only, and exclusively one thing, or serves one purpose. For instance, you can take a rock and bang it against another rock to make a knife. Eventually it will become perfect. It will become a knife.

Friends are like this. Yet, not all friends are stones used to better us. Some friends, if we took an honest inventory of our lives, don't make us a better person in any way. Some are just completely going in the opposite direction. The great wise king Solomon wrote in the book of Proverbs, "As iron sharpens iron, so one [person] sharpens another" (27:17). So if our goal in life is to become sharp iron, a person more connected to and like Jesus, then your friends should be iron as well. If we are iron and our friends are stone, the only thing that will come out of our relationship is a fire that's destined to destroy what has already shaped us for good.

Have you ever seen iron being smelted? When bits of raw iron, especially in the Iron Age and around the time Solomon lived, were mostly made into swords, they were put through a melting-hot fire. Through the process of burning the iron, it becomes malleable, ready to be shaped. Still today, iron smelters can take a hammer and shape iron into virtually any shape you want. When the iron cools down, that becomes its permanent shape. When iron is met with friction and fire again, it becomes loose and malleable again, ready to be shaped into something else. The only way to sharpen our sword is not through fire, but by another iron sword. Our friendships are no different.

A friend can be the difference between success and failure. They can be the difference between reaching our destination or detouring to some uncharted destination in life. Friends are meant to travel the road with us, not to carry the map or to drive the car. When we're headed in a particular direction, and start taking every detour our friends want to take, we'll either dramatically delay or never arrive at our desired destination.

> Friends are meant to travel the road with us, not to carry the map or to drive the car. When we're headed in a particular direction, and start taking every detour our friends want to take, we'll either dramatically delay or never arrive at our desired destination.

Friends have a tremendous capacity to influence the direction of our life. When it comes to the friends we have in life, they will either carry us to Jesus, like the paralytic man's friends, or carry us away.

Ultimately no one is more in control of who our friends are than we are. Who we surround ourselves with is our choice, and our choice tells the secret of what we really want in life. Jesus said it plainly, "Where your treasure is, there your heart will be also" (Matt. 6:21). Most times we think about that verse only when it comes to money, but really we can apply it to anything in life that takes whatever resource we have. Whether it be our money, our time, or our energy, wherever we spend the bulk of it is what we value most.

We can play dumb all we want and act innocent, but this is no epiphany. We are well aware of the friends we choose and what the motivations are for choosing them. We like them. We like what they do. We want to do what they do. The truth is that choosing friends who are headed in opposite directions shows a real lack of faith in God. We are saying that we are not convinced that God is able to give us the kind of friends that will be able to meet our needs. What our friendships tell us is what we really want in life.

Not only do our friendships tell us what we really want, but they also give us a clue to where we're headed. There was a kid in high school I knew who was always entrepreneurial. Every month he was selling some new merchandise. He sold everything from pagers to books to bubble gum. Whatever you needed, he had it. Not only did he have all kinds of products, he also had all kinds of money. I was impressed. I wanted to get to know him and be his friend. When I did, I was surprised by what I discovered. Everything he sold he either stole or got from someone who stole it. That wasn't the only discovery. I discovered that more of his money came from selling drugs than selling pagers. Where is he now? You probably guessed it right on the first try. Prison.

What saved me from diving into a deeper relationship with this guy wasn't that I was no longer impressed by his money. It was because I was more interested in staying out of prison. A friendship with this kid could have cost me a lot more than jail time. It could have cost me my life. I learned a valuable lesson in not maintaining a friendship with that guy. Unfortunately too many people fail to learn this simple principle: our choice in friends, good or bad, is a good indication of the direction our life is headed.

Who we surround ourselves with can make all the difference in our lives. But that difference depends on the kind of friends we choose. So it is not as much of a coin toss as you might have assumed. The friends we pick tell us a lot about what we want, and where we're headed, but also can act as the agents of change in directions that are good and beneficial to everyone.

Let's think about our life and our friends as a bank. We can only get out of the bank what we put in it. Friends have unparalleled access to make significant deposits into the bank of our life. What kinds of deposits do they make? Look at the outcome of our lives, or the "output" of our lives. Is what's coming out of us enough to position our lives for change?

If our lives are in need of real, authentic change, or healing, we need to be surrounded by friends with faith. You say,

"Does that mean I need to disregard the friends I already have?" Maybe we do. Maybe we don't need to disregard them as much as we need to distance ourselves from them. But a couple of things are certain, we become like the people we spend time with. And the friends we're surrounding ourselves with will either bring us closer to Christ or keep us away from Him.

It's time to kick a program of evaluation into high gear. There are four things that we need to identify in order to change the outputs of our lives:

- Friends that keep us away from Jesus.
- Places that steer our lives in the wrong direction.
- Relationships that prevent Jesus from being number one in our lives.
- Habits that prevent Christ from being exalted in us and through us.

Identify these four things in our life and change them. There is no way we can get high-quality outputs if we feed your lives with low-quality inputs. Think about who the people are who are making deposits into your life. The paralytic took inventory of his life. He had friends with faith who heard that Jesus was back in town, and because they were desperate to see life change, they did whatever it took to get their friend close to Jesus. The Scripture says, as was pointed out earlier, that Jesus saw *their* faith.

I never thought of faith as something we can see. But as it turns out, it really is. If we have true faith, people ought to be able to see it. Jesus' brother James knew what Jesus was talking about, and in a letter he wrote he says in James 2:18, "But someone will say, 'You have faith; I have deeds.' Show me your faith without deeds, and I will show you my faith by what I do." If someone has faith, we can really see it. What the paralytic was able to produce in his life was real faith that changed his life. All this because he chose to surround himself with friends who were full of faith, and that's what they poured and deposited into one another.

Your Surrender

I've read this story many times through the years, but I just realized something new about it. I learned that this man, this paralytic, wasn't only surrounded by friends with faith, but he was also surrendered to these friends. It isn't enough to just be around people or keep people around us who are people full of visible, real, tangible faith. We also need to open our lives to these friends and allow them to lead us and to make deposits into our lives as if our life was their very own.

You see, this man was paralyzed and he was fully dependent on these men. He didn't really have a choice when it came to getting into that house to see Jesus. He really had to allow himself to be completely free of controlling himself so that he could allow his faithful friends to use their own faith to help him. He had to be surrendered. In Mark 2:3 it says, "bringing to him a paralytic." When we look at the original language, we see that it is a present-tense verb that speaks of a continual action. We could literally translate it to mean, "bringing and kept on bringing the paralytic . . ."

In other words, they kept on bringing him until they could get him to Jesus because he was unable to take one step towards God on his own. He couldn't get to Jesus without them. And don't forget, they brought him, but he also allowed them to bring him. He saw the faith of those friends and he caught it. Their faith rubbed off on him and he wanted the hope that they had, the hope of Jesus, and the hope of life change.

Can you imagine how that conversation might have gone if he didn't also surrender himself to them? It would probably sound something like this, "Hey, we've been talking. We heard Jesus was coming back to town and we believe if we can get you to Him, that He can change your life. Now, it's not going to be easy, but with the four of us, we believe we can get you there." The paralytic might have responded something like this, "You know . . . I appreciate what you're trying to do, but I think I'll stay at home today. That's a tough trip, it's hot outside, *The Amazing Race* is on, and by the time we get there, Jesus will probably already be gone. After all, I can't walk . . . thanks anyway."

He had to be surrendered to them. The surrendered life says, "Yes, I'll accept the help, because I surely can't do it alone." Instead, he probably said something like this, "YES! Let's do it. Let me crawl on the pallet, you guys grab a corner, grab a rope, and let's go. I believe in you men! I believe you're right about Jesus. I've seen your faith and it has inspired me to have a faith of my own." Faithful friends make the difference! His faith was enough to get him from his house to the house where Jesus was. But it was his surrendering to their faith that lowered him through the roof where his life was changed.

Surrendering is by consent. It doesn't include kidnapping, or dragging, or forcing. Those friends didn't argue him to Jesus. They didn't have to trick or cajole him, they simply remained who he knew them to be all along. They had already proven to be trustworthy, faithful, dependable, and able. Friends like that are hard to come by. The paralytic proved to us that the quantity of friends you have doesn't really matter. He only needed a hand for each corner of his mat. What matters when it comes to being surrounded by and surrendered to those who hold the keys to the ignition of life change is quality. They brought him by consent and now he has positioned his life for change. They surrounded him and he surrendered to them because he trusted them and their faith had infected him.

Perhaps one of the most difficult things a person can do, especially among friends, is ask for help. But the truth is that friends should be the ones who automatically understand and are willing to help regardless of the circumstance or the complication. Yet, we don't often ask our friends for help when it comes to the deep, dark, secret needs we have because we don't want to appear weak. We don't want to be a burden, or for some, we don't have the kind of friends who could surround us and grab the corners of our mat. The paralytic experienced life change precisely because his needs were obvious. Only Jesus knew his heart and announced the forgiveness of his sins. Admitting our need for help, first to ourselves; then out loud to God; and finally to our trusted, faithful friends, can put our paralysis in life on the track for a marathon of life change.

> Perhaps one of the most difficult things a person can do, especially among friends, is ask for help. But the truth is that friends should be the ones who automatically understand and are willing to help.

How many tears had this man shed that no one recorded or maybe even knew? He might have had serious gut-wrenching nights of absolute despair where his tears dropped like rain. There was not only faith with his friends, but an intention and intensity of action that suggests strong feelings of desperation on their part. That means they really felt his pain too. That kind of feeling captures the meaning of compassion. Many times the Bible records that Jesus stretched out His hand to change someone's life because He was "moved with compassion."

They suffered with him. That is literally the definition of *compassion*. For this kind of intensity of action on their part must mean that when it all came down to it, the paralytic man bore his soul, his heart, and mind to these men. It shows that he was transparent. Or to put it another way, he was open, honest, and clear. There was no cover-up on his part, but rather a real conveyance of what he felt and hoped for that transferred to their hearts for him. That transfer of hope moved these men's feet and minds to creative action spurred by their own intense faith, and was seen through the plastic-wrap-like lens of transparency.

I think about the possibility that at some point he wanted to let up or give in and give up hope. Yet, because he was surrounded by them, and surrendered to them, and transparent with them, they also kept him accountable. Just imagine with me for a second that we have traveled all these miles with the last hope of being healed. We arrive at the destination only to be met with a virtually unending line wrapped around the building. Nightfall is fast approaching and we're convinced that there is no way Jesus will be able to see us. On top of that, we love our friends and can't stand to make them hold us up any longer. Dejected, we command them to take us back home. But no, they keep us accountable to our hope. They say, "Nope. You believed, we believed with you, and Jesus is going to see you this day, even if we have to break into someone's house to do it." That's accountability. These friends were committed to keep this man on the track of seeing his hopes come to reality no matter what it would take.

What many people in Jesus' day knew all too well in their tight-knit communities was the "sting of sin." They lived an existence everyday that reminded them that sin has a powerful effect on us all. Every day they walked trying to avoid the leper, passed the healing pools where the cripples reached to get in, avoided the alleyways of the blind, and avoided the dark corners where the demon-possessed spewed nonsense. They knew that sin had a real and tangible effect on a person's life. The paralytic was no different. Jesus acknowledged that his paralysis was caused by sin, so He said, "Son, your sins are forgiven" (Mark 2:5). We don't know whether this palsy was caused by a specific sin, or by the sin nature of humans, which causes so many other sicknesses and problems in the world. Yet the potency and power of sin remains, and so then does the need to be saved.

This paralytic man's healing came from Jesus' forgiveness. He was cleansed from the sin that kept him bedridden all those years. Jesus' words caused quite a stir among the religious rule checkers. They said, "You don't have power to do that. You can't forgive sins." Jesus told them they didn't know whom they were talking to and basically said, "You want proof that my simple words that you claim have no power work? Great, watch this, he's going to walk now." And in a tour de force, Jesus says the astonishing, "Get up, take your mat and go home" (Mark 2:11). They knew that sickness was a sign of sin. Not just universal sin of all humans, but of particular sins of individuals as well. Whatever the

> Whatever the case for this man, he was forgiven, healed, and changed forever thanks to friends who had faith enough to put him in a position where their faith caught the attention of the Healer.

case for this man, he was forgiven, healed, and changed forever thanks to friends who had faith enough to put him in a position where their faith caught the attention of the Healer.

In verse 12 of that same chapter it reads, "He got up, took his mat and walked out in full view of them all. This amazed everyone and they praised God, saying, 'We have never seen anything like this!'" Can you imagine this scene? This guy was jumping around, walking out of there carrying the mat he rode in on. It was without a doubt a remarkable scene. They even remarked, "We have never seen anything like this!" The man was saved and his life was changed forever.

Positioning our lives for change means fortifying ourselves in a wall of resistance. It means surrounding ourselves with influences that point us to Christ and surrendering when surrender seems impossible. A wall that is triple and quadruple enforced can withstand the cannons of confusion that life throws at us. It's resisting those arrows of hopelessness and backing them up with the might of a military and equipping us to fight with faith. When our strength runs dry, or we can no longer walk the last mile, or we're trying to get into the house, or beginning to lose focus or faith, these friends will pick up the four corners of our mat, remove the roof, and lower us into the hands of the One who forgives, heals, and saves. Remember . . .

- Your environment will determine your destination.
- Your inputs will determine your outputs.
- Surround yourself with friends with faith.
- Make sure your environments lead you to Jesus instead of keeping you away.

CHAPTER 4

The Touch That Changes Everything

Desperate times call for desperate measures

When I was a kid, we rode bikes. We played outside. And I know, most kids today would hear that and say, "Your parents must have been so mean! They made you play outside where the sun is shining and the air conditioning is nonexistent." It is mind-boggling to think that playing outside is becoming a thing of the past, but it really is. Not for us though. We played outside.

Where I grew up, everyone in my neighborhood thought they were professional BMX bikers. If you were to drive by my house after school let out, you would think you were at the X Games fan club practice facility. The kids in our neighborhood were serious when it came to this stuff.

One day we put our heads together and decided to build a bike ramp. This wasn't your everyday ramp by any means. We spent countless hours working in my neighbor's shop. My neighbor's dad had given us some scrap wood and some screws and then turned us loose. It was obvious that nobody in this group would grow up to be an engineer because the ramp was terrifying. It was about five feet off the ground, the legs were shaky, the angles were all wrong, and if we had to do it all over again, it would've probably been smart to see if it was level before calling the project complete. But even as questionable as the craftsmanship may have been, we decided to put it up and placed it in the middle of the street.

Now the big question amongst us was, "Who would go first?" Everyone was excited about the ramp when it was in the garage, but now that it was on the hot Texas pavement, the enthusiasm level seemed to have taken a tumble. I was tired of hearing the whining and the excuses, so I decided that I would go first.

It was intimidating as I sat on my bike, with one leg on the ground and the other shaking on the bike pedal. I envisioned the entire process. I would pedal strong for about forty yards, then evaluate my speed to make sure everything was just right, and then based off my evaluation, I would make adjustments before hitting the ramp. In my mind I was anticipating what my first trick would look like off this monster bike ramp, and I pictured what the reaction from all my buddies would be once I landed it.

I was mentally ready to make the jump. The time was right and I was ready. It was time to become a neighborhood legend.

The sequence of events looked a little different than I had imagined. It went something like this: I pedaled. I went too fast. I launched. I flew. I crashed. I bled. I cried like a baby.

Once I hit the ground, there was a huge gasp from my friends that came in unison, and it was so loud that I could hear it clearly through my own screaming and wailing. Everyone knew what this wipeout meant. It meant that we were probably going to get in trouble and we weren't going to be allowed to use the ramp anymore. Since nobody wanted to get in trouble, my friends tried to come to my aid. They began using their bottles of water and juice boxes to wash out my wounds, and it wasn't any help at all. They tried using their homework and random sheets of notebook paper to serve as a bandage and soak up the blood from my leg, but that didn't work either.

I was in pain and my leg was bleeding. It was embarrassing to cry like that in front of all my friends in my neighborhood, but the pain was overwhelming to the point that I didn't have control of it anymore. I was left there, lying in the street, bleeding and hurting, and then I heard a familiar voice. I looked out of the corner of my eye and saw my mom running to me. She had heard my cries and came out to help me.

Up to that point it was nothing but pain, crying, misery, and blood, but then she came out with a wet washrag and placed it on my leg. She whispered in my ear so that my friends couldn't hear, "Everything is going to be all right," and she was right because as soon as she placed the washrag on my leg, it seemed like all the pain went away. For me that day, it was my mom's touch that changed everything.

There have been multiple times that I've found myself in that very same situation in life; times when I've crashed and burned, times where I'm cut up and bleeding, times where I'm hurting and miserable, and times when it seems like all I can experience is pain.

And if I were a betting man, I'd bet that we've all been in a similar situation in our own lives. We know what that's like, don't we? We know what it's like to need a touch in our life to take away the pain and change our circumstance.

Throughout the pages of this book, we've already seen two people that could identify with this scenario: the leper and the paralytic. It's apparent that if we look at these individuals we would say, "There's no way they can change. There's no way the outcomes of these circumstances are going to change." Well, they did. In fact, not only did their lives change, but also their souls were saved. And again, it happened when they came into a new relationship that inspired and sustained their hope. From that new relationship they received a new way of thinking. And from that new way of thinking, change came! Now, let's look at a sick and dying twelve-year-old little girl.

In Mark 5:22–23, we read where a man named Jairus, a desperate dad, came seeking Jesus in order to help his daughter who was sick and dying. The Bible tells us that Jesus went with Jairus back to his house where his daughter remained and was near death. Now do you remember what happened along the way? They were interrupted. Do you remember who interrupted them and what happened? Well, we read about it beginning in verse 25:

> And a woman was there who had been subject
> to bleeding for twelve years. She had suffered
> a great deal under the care of many doctors

and had spent all she had, yet instead of getting better she grew worse. When she heard about Jesus, she came up behind him in the crowd and touched his cloak, because she thought, "If I just touch his clothes, I will be healed." Immediately her bleeding stopped and she felt in her body that she was freed from her suffering. At once Jesus realized that power had gone out from him. He turned around in the crowd and asked, "Who touched my clothes?" "You see the people crowding against you," his disciples answered, "and yet you can ask, 'Who touched me?'" But Jesus kept looking around to see who had done it. Then the woman, knowing what had happened to her, came and fell at his feet and, trembling with fear, told him the whole truth. He said to her, "Daughter, your faith has healed you. Go in peace and be freed from your suffering." (vv. 25–34)

It's pretty obvious that the common thread between all of the people we've met in this book has been the fact that they were desperate for change. This lady had undergone an incredible journey and had reached the point of desperation. Imagine the audacity of this woman, reaching out and grabbing hold of the garment of Jesus. She was courageous, but we'll discover that her courage was a step that led her to the life change she so desperately needed.

Her Condition

This lady had a condition and it was a serious problem. And we can probably relate. Perhaps not to this specific problem, but we know what it's like to be in a condition of suffering, pain, and misery.

We know what it's like to hurt and we understand the devastation of knowing that the pain isn't going away any time soon. This lady had a serious condition and she had suffered from it for quite some time, but let's examine what this condition meant for her.

A person in her condition was excommunicated from the temple and the synagogue according to the Law of Moses (Lev. 15). If that wasn't bad enough, according to the Law of the Rabbis, she was divorced from her husband, shut out from family life, and ostracized by society.

For the past twelve years of her life, she had been living in total isolation with no family, no friends, no touch, no corporate worship, and no hope for change. But we need to notice not only the extent of her suffering, but the expense of her suffering as well.

> She had suffered a great deal under the care
> of many doctors and had spent all she had, yet
> instead of getting better she grew worse.

In Dr. Luke's account of this story in Luke 8, he tells us in verse 43 that she had "spent all her livelihood on physicians and could not be healed by any." She not only had a health problem, but now she had a financial problem.

The length of her suffering was for twelve years and the loss of her suffering was that she had spent all of her money on doctors and "could not be healed by any."

No man could change her condition. No doctor could change her condition. And Mark tells us in verse 26 that her condition "grew worse." She wasn't getting better, but on the contrary, she was becoming worse. She was deemed incurable. She could not be healed.

That was her condition. It was a hopeless condition and one that left her in isolation. It was a condition that left her broke and without any chance of a doctor or healer changing her life.

Her Confidence

When your circumstances are as grim as this, it's nearly impossible to have a confident spirit or attitude. When you're in a hopeless condition, it's nearly impossible to have hope.

This lady found herself in a helpless and hopeless position and despite her condition she still had confidence. In verse 27 it says, "When she heard about Jesus . . ."

At first glance that doesn't sound like much, but it really is a big deal. She heard about Jesus, which tells us that she would have never come to Jesus had she not heard about Him first. That tells us that somebody somewhere talked to her about Jesus and planted that seed in her heart and because she had heard about Him, she began to believe in Him and have confidence that He could change her life.

But not only did she hear, it also says, she "touched."

> When she heard about Jesus, she came up
> behind him in the crowd and touched his cloak,
> because she thought, "If I just touch his clothes,
> I will be healed." (v. 28)

Now don't think that she just lightly touched His garment. This word translated "touched" speaks of an action of force. You can say that she "clutched or grasped" His garment. In her desperation, she aggressively grabbed hold of Jesus as if she would never let go. She came from behind Jesus and grabbed onto those tassels and verse 29 tells us that: "Immediately her bleeding stopped and she felt in her body that she was freed from her suffering."

We need to learn something about her touch before we continue because it would be misleading to believe that all we have to do is reach out and touch Jesus today and all our problems will disappear. For her, it wasn't just an instantaneous touch. Her clutching of His garment was more than a touch; it was a touch of faith! It was her faith that directed her to Jesus and it was her faith that delivered her. It requires faith to reach out to Jesus! She learned that day that reaching out to Jesus by faith can bring physical healing, but not only physical healing, it can also bring emotional healing. And not only can this faith bring you physical and emotional healing, but it can lead you to spiritual healing as well.

This lady was made whole that day after touching the hem of Jesus' garment. She was made physically whole, emotionally whole, and spiritually whole! Her healing, which was once incomprehensible, was now complete. That which was once impossible was made possible because of the power of Jesus working in her life. Many times we want to end the story here. We like to land on these incredible stories of faith and harbor on the physical healings and evidences brought by the miracles. But there's another level of faithfulness that

> Her journey with Jesus didn't end in her enjoying and being thankful for the physical blessing from God . . . Her confidence in Jesus led to her becoming complete in Jesus.

this lady experienced that went beyond the miracle she experienced. Her journey with Jesus didn't end in her enjoying and being thankful for the physical blessing from God, even though she was thankful for it. Her confidence in Jesus led to her becoming complete in Jesus, and once she had experienced Him firsthand, it led to her confession.

Her Confession

Have you ever tapped someone on the shoulder and acted like it wasn't you? It makes them wonder, "Who touched me?" Right? I do that to my kids all the time. I'll tap them on the shoulder and walk away or look the other direction, and every time they'll respond by saying, "Who touched me?" When you're the one getting touched, it gets frustrating.

Jesus wasn't frustrated here. It says in verse 30: "At once Jesus realized that power had gone out from him. He turned around in the crowd and asked, 'Who touched my clothes?'"

When we read that, it can almost seem like He was frustrated, but He wasn't even asking the question because He was curious or didn't know the answer. Jesus said, "Who touched me?" to give this lady an opportunity to confess. He asked the question in public to give her an opportunity to make a public statement of faith.

And this is very interesting because at the moment this lady was healed, Jesus required an open confession on the spot. There wasn't any lag time. He didn't give her time to make her list of pros and cons for confessing Jesus. It was her time to decide who Jesus was going to be in her life and Jesus knew that what came out of her mouth was going to be a reflection of what was in her heart.

> But Jesus kept looking around to see who had done it. Then the woman, knowing what had happened to her, came and fell at his feet and, trembling with fear, told him the whole truth. (vv. 32–33)

Why would Jesus require an open confession on the spot like that? The reason was because He had a blessing for her and many times, in order for God to bless us, He first wants a confession from us.

> He said to her, "Daughter, your faith has healed you. Go in peace and be freed from your suffering." (v. 34)

He said, "Go in peace," and when you look at this phrase in the original language it actually translates to mean, "Go *into* peace." There's a big difference in the two statements. In John 14:27 it says:

> Peace I leave with you; my peace I give you. I
> do not give to you as the world gives. Do not let
> your hearts be troubled and do not be afraid.

This lady had experienced the touch that changes everything and now she could "go into peace." For the first time in twelve years, this lady was going to experience peace. After all of the hurt and all the pain she finally had the chance to do something that was once considered unthinkable.

She entered into peace knowing she was no longer excommunicated from the temple. She was no longer ostracized from her family. She would no longer be considered unclean in society and no longer be in bondage to her past.

Jesus required an open confession because He had a special blessing for her. But also so that others might believe. When we are willing to confess what Jesus has done in our life, it helps others see Him more clearly and it helps others come to Him. And the truth is that we don't do this enough. We, as the church and the body of Christ, don't confess what Jesus has done in our life enough. But when we do, it helps others come to Jesus and it helps others have a greater faith in Him.

There's another reason that Jesus required an open confession that day: to encourage Jairus! Remember him? This woman had caused Jesus to stop on His way to Jairus's home where his sick and dying daughter was. Jesus hit the pause button on this desperate dad in order to address the needs of this lady. And the entire time, Jairus stood by Jesus' side and had the best seat in the house as he watched the power of God at work.

There stood Jairus, anxiously waiting for Jesus to get to his house before it was too late. We read in verse 33 that she, knowing what had happened to her, came and fell at Jesus' feet and, trembling with fear, told Him the whole truth. Can't you hear Jairus thinking to himself at first, *Come on!! Make it quick! We've got to get to my house* now! *My daughter is sick and dying.*

And as Jairus heard the whole story about her having this "flow of blood" for twelve years I can imagine that his ears began to perk up. After hearing of how her touching the hem of the garment of Jesus healed her, I'm sure he started thinking, *If Jesus can heal this woman who has had this problem for twelve years, that means that He can heal my twelve-year-old daughter too.*

Her confession strengthened the faith of Jairus. Her confession also brought her a special blessing: "Daughter, your faith has healed you."

Faith directed her to Jesus and faith delivered her! Hebrews 11:6 says, "Without faith it is impossible to please Him." Jesus saw her faith and told this lady, "Go [into] peace and be freed from your suffering."

What happened to this woman reminds me of what David tells us in Psalm 50:15, "Call upon Me in the day of trouble; I will deliver you, and you shall glorify Me" (NKJV). Reaching out to Jesus brings peace on the inside and praise on the outside.

This story reminded me of what it was like to be lying there in the street that day—bleeding, crying, miserable, embarrassed, and in pain. It was excruciating, but the misery ended once I experience the touch of my mom.

That may describe in a sense where you find your own life today. When you look in a mirror, you may see someone who is hurting and desperate for change. If so, understand that no matter what the pain you're currently experiencing may be, there is a touch that changes everything. That's not to say that we will never experience hardship because that is never promised. However, we are guaranteed that no matter what we go through or what circumstances we may endure, that they will never be too big for God. He'll always walk through tough times with us. He'll always give us the strength to endure. God will never put us through

> We are guaranteed that no matter what we go through or what circumstances we may endure, that they will never be too big for God. He'll always walk through tough times with us. He'll always give us the strength to endure.

something that we aren't capable of getting through with Him by our side.

Are you in need of that touch today? If so, be aggressive. Be assertive. Be willing to reach out and grab hold of Jesus. Once you do, never let go.

CHAPTER 5

It's Never Too Late for Change

Where to go when change is needed

To most people, *change* is a dirty word. Many of us won't admit that change is a dirty word, but it is. We say we're okay with change, but at the same time, we sit in the exact same seat every single Sunday and wouldn't know what to do if we were forced to sit somewhere else. We wear the same cologne or perfume that we have always worn. We have the same friends, eat at the same restaurants, and have the same conversations with the same people about the same old things. It's fashionable to say that we're okay with change, but the reality is that many of us despise the very thought of it. There's just something about *changing* that doesn't sound appealing to us at all. Most of the time, we're okay with things just the way they are, and we don't want to change.

For the Christmas holiday this year, my family made the trip to Atlanta to be with my parents. Not only were my parents in Atlanta, but also in attendance were my brother and his family, my sister and her family, and my uncle and his family. Seventeen people under the same roof, and seven of them were children. At one point of the visit, I found myself sitting on the couch, completely entertained by the sideshow that was going on at my feet. There were four little babies, my nieces and nephews, and they were having a blast interacting with one another, making noises toward each other and responding as only a little baby could respond. It was hilarious to watch.

In watching them play, I was reminded of the times when my own kids were babies on the floor. As I was reflecting on those times, all of a sudden a terrible odor hit the room. It felt like my nose was on fire! One of these cute little kids had just made a deposit in its diaper, but you'd never know by looking at them. All four babies continued playing. They continued making cute noises and responding to one another. From first glance, you would never know that one of them was sitting on something gross, but it was apparent by the foul aroma that one of them had to be. About that time, the moms picked up on the smell and began investigating—picking the babies up one at a time and smelling their backsides. (As a side note, moms are some of the smartest people I've ever known, but their technique doesn't seem very wise for whatever reason—sticking your nose in a place where you know that the smell is going to be bad.) Anyway, after picking up a few kids and offering a few sniffs, the smelly baby was identified. Now, at this point, the baby was fine; still happy, smiling, and making cute baby noises and faces, but the moment the mom began trying to change the baby's diaper, the baby began turning on her. It didn't matter if it was gross, and it didn't

> The moment the mom began trying to change the baby's diaper, the baby began turning on her. It didn't matter if it was gross, and it didn't matter if it stunk, the baby didn't want anything to do with being changed.

matter if it stunk, the baby didn't want anything to do with being changed. It was completely fine and didn't appear to feel the need to be changed.

In the midst of my entertainment, as I watched this episode occur, I was reminded of the times when I've had something in my life that stinks, and I was completely okay with it. I reflected on the times when I was running from God; when I was living in complete sin and disobedience to

God, and I was completely fine with things just the way they were. Perhaps we all know what it's like to need change, but have no desire for change.

Even as adults, we don't like change most of the time. We're okay with things the way they are.

But on the other hand, there are other times when we realize that something stinks in our lives. We recognize that a change needs to take place. We look at our lives, or the lives of a friend or loved one, and we say, "Something has got to change, and it has to change *now*, or the outcome is going to be very bad!" Typically when we get to that point, we identify the change that needs to take place, and we try our very best to change it.

This is a dangerous place to be, because all of the sudden, we've moved into the role of being a "change agent," and we've already discovered that we are typically incapable of instigating lasting life change in our lives or the lives of our friends or loved ones. But when desperation sets in and we assume this role, what we're communicating through our position is that we know change needs to happen and we feel as though we can fix the situation.

I don't know about you, but things get different when I'm fighting for a loved one or when I'm fighting for a friend. When I get to a point where I've begged God to change the heart of someone I love, or in my desperation I've implored God to move in their lives, it's like a switch is flipped and I all of the sudden become a salesman. And now, as a sales-man, I'm going to convince you that you need to change. As a salesman, I am going to begin selling you on how you can change your life and what steps you can take to be different or make different choices.

When we assume the role of "change agent" and begin trying to change the people we love, we typically have three tactics that we like to use that we believe will instigate life change.

1. *Facts:* We believe that if we offer enough evidences or enough statistics, that ultimately this person is going to recognize that change needs to take place.
2. *Fear:* We believe that if we scare this individual bad enough that they will acknowledge the neces-sary change that needs to take place and, therefore, change.
3. *Force:* We believe that by using our position or plat-form, we can demand change and enforce it by using our authority.

These three tactics we use have something in common. All of them may lead to a temporary change, but none of them will lead to lasting life change.

As we were spending time with the family, my brother asked me how we potty trained our kids. I honestly couldn't remember. My response was a typical "dad" response, "Just don't let them drink anything after lunch." After thinking through it, this was probably bad advice.

How did we potty train our kids? I really couldn't remember what we did. It's obviously easier to potty train a child while they're awake than to wait until they're asleep, but for some reason, I couldn't recall the things we did to move towards that milestone.

What if we would have used these three tactics to try to get our kids to quit wetting the bed? Do you think we could prompt change in the life of our kids by using these methods?

What if we began by telling them all about the **facts**? "Only 5.7 percent of five-year-olds actually still wet the bed! Do you really want to be in the fifth percentile?" Something tells me that facts aren't going to move our kids towards change.

What if we used **fear**? "If you wet the bed tonight, there's going to be some terrible consequence in the morning. You better not wet the bed! If you do, you're going to wish you never went to sleep!" Do you think fear will direct your kids toward change? Your kids will wet the bed before they even go to sleep!

What if we tried **force**? "You will not wet the bed! You won't! I, as your father, in all of my authority forbid you to pee in your pants!" It's not going to work.

It's understandable that we want to see our friends or loved ones change. It's understandable that we tend to "sell" or lead them towards the change that we know they need, but facts, fear, and force won't bring lasting life change to a bed wetter—or anyone, for that matter.

Perhaps you're reading this today and thinking, *Then what am I supposed to do?* Maybe you have a child that is in complete rebellion today—rebellion against the family, against the church, or even against God. They may be running away from God today, living a lifestyle that is a disappointment any way you look at it, and you're wondering, *What am I supposed to do? Where am I supposed to go?*

You may have a friend or a loved one that hates God or hates the church. You've prayed for their salvation, but they want nothing to do with it and you're stuck asking, "Is it too late for them?"

It's never too late.

Keep praying. Keep begging God to work a miracle and believe that He's capable of it.

Trust the Process—Pray for Progress

If you want to experience lasting life change, you can't use tactics, you've got to trust the process and pray for progress. God wants to change hearts; He wants to turn lives towards Him. Sometimes we forget that change isn't something we can cook up, but it's the result of what takes place in someone's heart, mind, and soul.

And that's why we have to trust the process and pray for progress. It's not facts, fear, and force that lead people to change, it's people having faith that are willing to place their hope in Jesus, the Change Agent.

Many of us know what it's like to pray for someone over and over again, asking God for a miracle—asking Him for life change—and it seems like God's not even listening because the person you're petitioning for seems to be slipping through the cracks faster and faster. That is a frustrating place to be, when you're looking at someone that was once spiritually wounded and now it seems as if they have spiritually flatlined. It's hard to pray for someone that is spiritually dead because it's like your prayers are hitting the ceiling and bouncing back!

> Many of us know what it's like to pray for someone over and over again, asking God for a miracle—asking Him for life change—and it seems like God's not even listening.

When I was eight years old, my dad came home from work one day and made the pronouncement, "Hey kids, I bought you something today." With excitement, all three of us lined up to see what it was he bought. About that time from behind his back, he presented each of us with our very own baby chicken. At first I was confused, but then he explained that it was almost Easter and he thought it would be fun for us to get some chicks. For whatever reason, we were thrilled! My dad was overjoyed in giving them to us. The one person that was less than happy was my mom. Apparently my dad hadn't talked this one through with her before making the big purchase (which was a shock to me because I thought husbands always communicated clearly with their wives!). As they were discussing the details, we kids were naming our chickens. I decided to name mine "Buffalo Wing."

Mom called all of us kids together and said, "You can keep the chicks, but I have just one rule: no chickens in the house!" We agreed and went to play with our Easter birds.

About three days later, it was Saturday afternoon and Dad was home with us so my mom could grab a few groceries for the week. That day just so happened to be one of the worst thunderstorms in that city's history as well.

Our house was on top of a hill and at the bottom of our property was a creek. We didn't have to worry about flooding, but the chickens did. My dad built their coop right next to the creek, so as the water fell from the sky, the water began rising from the creek. As the water began threatening the baby chickens in their coop, my dad made a quick decision to put on his swimsuit and wade into the water and rescue them from the flood.

He made his way back to the back porch with the chickens in his shirt, where I was there waiting for him. He looked at me and asked, "What should we do now?" I responded, "I don't know. I'm an eight-year-old boy!" He was looking for more than that, so he asked me again, "What should we do with the chickens?" In all of my confusion, I said, "Take them inside?" He said, "YES! Great idea! Remember that this was *your* idea!" And we brought the chickens in the house.

Once they were inside, they went crazy! There were chickens on top of the refrigerator. Chickens were flying into the walls. One chicken even made a deposit on the kitchen counter. We knew that something had to be done or we were all going to die as soon as Mom walked into the house. Dad quickly gathered the chickens up, walked to the garage door, and threw them into the garage where he knew they would be dry and safe.

I soon realized the reason my mom wasn't excited about our new Easter chicks. It wasn't that she hated chickens. It was the fact that we already had so many animals. You see, about three weeks prior, my dog had six puppies. So now, we had a total of seven dogs, living in a plastic swimming pool, and this "puppy pool" was located in the garage.

This realization completely slipped our minds when Dad threw the chickens into the garage. Nobody thought twice about it for several hours, but once we did, my dad made his way to the garage to check on the chicks. He looked to the left and saw my sister's chick. He looked to the right and saw my brother's chick. He searched the entire garage but couldn't find Buffalo Wing. Finally, he made his way to the puppy pool and there it was. My Easter chick made his way to the pool and was greeted by six hungry puppies. They chewed him up and spit him out. He wasn't dead, but as my dad observed him, he knew that it was in bad shape. He called me over and warned me for the worst. He tried everything he could to keep Buffalo Wing alive (everything except mouth-to-beak) and as he was working on my chick, I remember praying that God would keep my chicken alive. "God, please don't let my baby chicken die," I prayed. I begged God to save its life, but after about an hour, my dad informed me that the chicken had died.

I know that's a silly illustration, but for an eight-year-old boy, that was a tough lesson I learned that day.

I learned that God's timing is different from our timing. I learned that He sees things differently than we do. I learned that even when we pray to God and beg God to work a miracle, there are times He says "yes," times He says "no," and times He says "not yet." But at the same time, I rec-ognize that He's God, and ultimately He knows what's best.

In this chapter, we're going to look at a man in the book of Mark that learned a little about Jesus as well. He was a dad that was desperate for change. You see, he didn't have a wounded baby chicken, he had a twelve-year-old little girl that was sick and dying, and more than anything, he wanted someone to heal her body and change her life.

> When Jesus had again crossed over by boat to the other side of the lake, a large crowd gath-ered around him while he was by the lake. Then one of the synagogue rulers, named Jairus, came there. Seeing Jesus, he fell at his feet and pleaded earnestly with him, "My little daughter is dying. Please come and put your hands on her so that she will be healed and live." So Jesus went with him. A large crowd followed and pressed around him. (Mark 5:21–24)

This dad desired life change for his little girl and throughout this story, we are going to peek in on the process that he went through in order to get the change he so desired.

He Recognized His Need for Change

This man Jairus looked at this circumstance and he understood that he wasn't capable of saving his daughter. And that's a terrible feeling for a dad; it's a humbling place to be when you're looking at one of your kids and you realize there is nothing you can do to make it better. It's a feeling of complete helplessness, but that's the place Jairus found himself. This was a situation that was beyond him. It was bigger than him and he wasn't capable of changing anything.

That's why he went to Jesus. Somehow, and for some reason, there was no doubt in the mind of Jairus that Jesus could heal his daughter. Maybe he had heard about Jesus healing the leper, or perhaps he had heard about the demon-possessed man. We don't know, but what we do know is that this dad had confidence that Jesus could change the circumstance and heal his little girl.

He Asks Jesus for Life Change

> . . . and pleaded earnestly with him, "My little daughter is dying. Please come and put your hands on her so that she will be healed and live." (Mark 5:23)

He didn't just desire change; he was desperate for change to take place. He was desperate for Jesus to heal his daughter.

He wasn't embarrassed to ask Jesus. He wasn't too prideful to approach him. He wasn't worried about offending anyone or making a fool out of himself. *He was desperate*—and we've learned that when you're desperate for life change, it changes the rules. It changes the whole game and at that point, nothing else matters. This dad was desperate.

More than a Father, He Was an Advocate for Change

Jairus recognized his need for change. He was desperate for his daughter's healing and he asked Jesus for it. That is his position up to this point, but at the same time, we can't overlook his daughter's perspective in the story. You may not be the one asking God to help someone else, but you may be the one seeking change for yourself. Like this daughter, you may be the one who is in need of healing today. You may be the one in need of a miracle or healing or the touch of God in your life.

Let me tell you what she needed in order for life change to occur, because it's the same thing we need when we find our lives in need of change: she needed an advocate.

She needed someone to plead her case to Christ. She needed an advocate to represent her and go before her and, just as she had an advocate in her father, we have an advocate today with Jesus.

> My dear children, I write this to you so that you
> will not sin. But if anybody does sin, we have
> one who speaks to the Father in our defense—
> Jesus Christ, the Righteous One. (1 John 2:1)

> This is love: not that we loved God, but that he
> loved us and sent his Son as an atoning sacrifice
> for our sins. (1 John 4:10)

This twelve-year-old little girl had no chance for change without an advocate and neither do we. What her father was for her, Jesus is for us.

This is a powerful part of the story because when this father approaches Jesus and asks Him for change, we see Jesus respond with action. It says in Mark 5:24, "So Jesus went with him." When the father approaches Him in his desperation, we see the Son of God go with him. That should tell us something about Jesus today. It tells us that He goes where He's wanted. When He sees His children desperate and pleading, He doesn't refuse to go, He goes where He's wanted. And He'll go with us if we seek Him.

Amos 5:6 says, "Seek the Lord and live . . ." (NKJV). He goes where He's wanted, and those who seek Him always find Him.

Amos 5:6 says, "Seek the Lord and live . . ." (NKJV). He goes where He's wanted, and those who seek Him always find Him. Jesus said it Himself in Jeremiah 29:13, "You will seek me and find me when you seek me with all your heart."

So this dad is seeking Jesus. He recognizes his need for change, and then he asks Jesus for it. He was an advocate for his daughter, and Jesus, being the advocate He is, goes with the man to see his little girl. But as the story continues, something strange and unexpected happens in this father's process to finding life change.

He Waits on Jesus for Change

As they're headed towards the little girl, I'm sure Jairus is leading the way. He's probably walking at the fastest pace he'd ever walked because of the urgency he was feeling. In the midst of their journey, with Jairus leading Jesus, Jesus decides to stop and heal a lady that needed healing. Imagine the thoughts going through his mind at this point. They're walking quickly from point A to point B, where his daughter lay dying in a bed, and this father is trying his best to get there as fast as possible, but then Jesus hits the pause button and chooses to address this lady's need along the way—all while this Dad stood by and observed.

Jairus is just standing there, waiting and watching, probably anxious and nervous, and all the while, he's standing there watching Jesus heal this woman. And even though the pause at first probably made him crazy, I'm sure it also caused his faith to grow, seeing the power of God at work

At first, I'm sure Jairus was thinking, *Come on Jesus, we're running out of time.* You see, his timing probably looked a little different from Jesus' timing at that point, but what we can learn from this is that pauses don't take God by surprise. There's a purpose in every pause. And even when you find yourself waiting on Jesus, we've got to remember that when we're waiting on God and waiting with God, we aren't wasting our time.

Jairus waited on Jesus and his faith grew. He found his trust in Jesus growing while he was waiting. It was during the pause that he got to see Jesus do something supernatural and heal a woman. Again, there's a purpose in every pause. So, understand that when we find ourselves waiting on Jesus, the pause we are experiencing is not a surprise to our God. It's His plan.

Let's be honest. This sounds great. It sounds like everything in life is going to be good now. We recognize when and where change is needed. We ask Jesus for the change. He's our advocate, we wait on him . . . it sounds like a fairy tale where everything in the process turns out great.

But look what happens as Jairus is waiting on Jesus:

> While Jesus was still speaking, some men came
> from the house of Jairus, the synagogue ruler.
> "Your daughter is dead," they said. "Why
> bother the teacher anymore?" (Mark 5:35)

After all his efforts, and all his prayers, and all his wait-ing, and with Jesus by his side, on the way to his daughter, they get word that his daughter had died.

She's dead.

Death has a certain finality to it. It's the end. It's all over, and when something is all over, when it's done, there is no more hope. Jairus at this point had lost all hope. His daugh-ter was dead, the circumstance was hopeless, and there was nothing he as her father could do about it.

At this point, I'm certain he was thinking, *It's too late! It's too late for change!* He felt completely and utterly hopeless.

Imagine his reactions at the mention of her death. His hope was gone and he must have been completely crushed. Imagine the anger he must have felt. He was probably angry with himself for waiting so long to go to Jesus. He must have felt anger towards Jesus for hitting the pause button and healing the lady along the journey. He may have felt anger towards the lady he healed for being the distraction that prevented Jesus from making it back in time. He had to be angry. He had to be overcome with disappointment and resentment and bitterness and doubt. He probably doubted

Jesus' deity from the moment the man said, "Your daughter is dead." He was asking questions like, "How could this man Jesus allow something like this to happen?" She was dead and all hope was gone.

That's just a miserable place to be. Maybe we can relate to Jairus today. Perhaps you know someone, someone you've been praying for a long time and they are spiritually flat-lined. You can remember when there was hope and they were spiritually limping along, but now when you look at them and their rebellion and their disobedience, you see them as being spiritually dead and as far as you're concerned, there isn't any hope and it's just a little too late.

You know what it's like to give of your time and energy and effort and resources and for whatever reason, they've continued to disappoint you and run away from you. You know what it's like to pray for someone and nothing seems to happen. You've waited on Jesus and waited on Jesus and waited on Jesus, and then get to the point where you throw your hands in the air and scream, "What's the point? They're spiritually dead!" You can relate to Jairus.

But you see, as we keep reading, we discover that Jairus learns something that we need to learn as well. He learned that not only does Jesus have authority over disease, but He also has authority over death.

His Instruction

Even bad news can become good news when Jesus is in it.

> Ignoring what they said, Jesus told the syna-
> gogue ruler, "Don't be afraid; just believe."
> (Mark 5:36)

Those are both commands from Jesus. Command 1: *Don't be afraid!* In other words, stop worrying! Stop fearing! Stop it! You say, "With everything I'm facing, how could I stop being afraid?" He answers that question with Command 2: *Just Believe!*

> It's a fact that you can't trust and fear. You can't trust while you're afraid, and you can't be afraid while you're trusting. When trust moves in, fear moves out.

How do I stop fearing? Just believe. To *just* believe means to "not do anything other than believe." To *believe* means to "trust." It's a fact that you can't trust and fear. You can't trust while you're afraid, and you can't be afraid while you're trusting. When trust moves in, fear moves out. When fear moves in, trust moves out. Jesus said, "Don't be afraid; just believe."

His Separation

> He did not let anyone follow him except Peter,
> James and John the brother of James. (Mark 5:37)

I find it interesting that Jesus didn't allow the curious seekers to approach the house with Him. He just took the trusted three.

It's says in verse 38, "When they came to the home of the synagogue ruler, Jesus saw a commotion, with people crying and wailing loudly."

Matthew tells us in his account that there were flute players playing (Matt. 9:23). At this point in history and in this particular culture, it was customary to have professional mourners present when someone was getting close to death. That way when the person died, there were people there, playing music, weeping, and leading in the mourning process.

In Mark 5:39–40, Jesus addresses these people and says, "'Why make this commotion and weep? The child is not dead, but sleeping.' And they ridiculed Him" (NKJV). They laughed at Him and made fun of Him for saying that the girl wasn't dead but only sleeping. They had seen the girl die. They knew that she was dead and didn't believe in what Jesus was insinuating or suggesting.

Don't miss this part. Jesus removed all of those who didn't believe from the house. Only believers remained. Those who ridiculed Jesus, made fun of Him, and didn't believe in Him missed out on the miracle that day, just like they do still today.

His Observation

What they saw wasn't what Jesus saw. His observation looked a lot different from their observation! They saw a dead girl. He saw a sleeping girl. They saw a hopeless situation. Jesus saw a hopeful situation. They saw a problem. He saw a platform for a potential miracle.

That's what problems are. They are platforms for God to work miracles. When He sees a problem in your life, He sees something that has the potential of being changed for His glory and your good. If the man never had leprosy, Jesus would have never healed him. If the lady had never bled, Jesus wouldn't have been able to stop the bleeding. And if this young girl had never died, Jesus would have never been able to raise her from the dead.

Your problems are platforms for God to work miracles. And once we understand that, we'll be able to praise Him through our problems. God doesn't see things like we do. He sees the big picture. He sees the end result. He sees how the movie of our life plays out. We see one frame at a time. That's why it's so important for us to trust God and just believe.

His Declaration

So the man came from the house of Jairus, approached Jairus and Jesus, and declared that his daughter was dead. After experiencing the terror of the moment, Jesus and Jairus made their way to the house. Once they arrived, they saw the young girl lying lifeless on the bed and Jesus reached out to her.

> He took her by the hand and said to her, "*Talitha koum!*" (which means, "Little girl, I say to you, get up!") Immediately the girl stood up and walked around (she was twelve years old). At this they were completely astonished. (Mark 5:41–42)

She stood up and walked around. This is the same girl that was lifeless just moments ago. This girl was flatlined. She was dead, and now she is alive! And yet, the parents thought it was too late for a miracle. Their hope was gone. They had given up. Jesus said, "Girl, get up!" and she did! She was dead and then made alive!

What they realized was that it's never too late when God is involved. Jesus said in Matthew 19:26, "With God all things are possible."

There they were: Jesus, Jairus, the mother of the child, Peter, James, and John, as well as the lifeless body of this twelve-year-old little girl in an atmosphere of faith, and Jesus speaks to the girl in her native language saying, "*Talitha koum*" meaning, "Little girl, I say to you, get up!" He asked the girl to do the impossible, and with His command came the power to make it possible. And it says in verse 42, "Immediately the girl stood up and walked around. At this they were completely astonished."

It's never too late to change! Not as long as Jesus is still on the throne. Not as long as He's in charge.

It's never too late to change! Not as long as Jesus is still on the throne. Not as long as He's in charge. It's never too late! And that needs to be something that we believe today. As long as there is a heartbeat, there's still hope and sometimes even without a heartbeat, Jesus isn't through working yet.

Don't give up. Don't stop praying. Don't stop asking. Stay on your knees. Stay on your face. Stay in the Word and remember that the God you serve isn't taken by surprise by your circumstances, and He's big enough and capable enough to help you through them.

You want to see life change happen? Don't use tactics. Facts, fear, and force won't lead to lasting life change, but you know what does? Faith.

Trust the process. Pray for progress. And never give up hope.

CHAPTER 6

Change That Leads to Freedom

Escaping the cage and experiencing freedom

The mall at Christmastime is one of the most frightening places on the planet. Last Christmas my family ventured out to the local galleria in mid-December and it really was terrifying. The parking lots were packed and everyone seemed to be upset about something. People were hurrying and scurrying through the crowded corridors, trying to find their last-minute gifts, and all the while my wife and I were gloating because we had completed our shopping for the year. We grabbed the hands of our kids and made our way through the food court, all the way to the North Pole where Santa sat in front of a line of about a hundred children waiting to sit in his lap. After the longest forty-five minutes of my kids' lives, it was finally their turn to see the big man in person. They ran up to him and jumped on his lap. He struck up the conversation by asking them the token Santa questions: First of all, "Have you been a good boy and a good girl this year?" My kids of course answered, "Yes," which was a questionable response, but we let it slide. The second question he asked was, "What do you want for Christmas this year?" And the response was one that we were not prepared for. Up to this point, they had asked for scooters and mp3 players, and now they are looking at Santa, nose-to-nose, and responding in a simultaneous fashion, "We want a puppy!"

We weren't prepared for that at all. We love dogs, but we thought we were finished with the dog phase in our family. When our children were younger, we gave our dog to an elderly couple because we didn't want our babies crawling on a floor covered with dog hair—and now the kids were asking Santa to make that a reality in our world again.

After much consideration, I finally came to terms with the idea. We were getting a dog. But I also wanted to make sure that my opinion was heard in regards to what kind of dog we would get. I wasn't real picky on the breed, but I just didn't want one of those embarrassing yippy dogs. I didn't want a dog that would wear clothes and fit in a purse. I wanted a manly dog, and I pleaded my case in hopes that Santa would grant my wish.

Well, Christmas morning rolled around. The kids woke up early and began screaming so that everyone in the house would know that Christmas had officially begun. We rolled out of bed, grabbed the camera, and made our way to the living room where we found presents laid out and displayed by the fireplace mantel. One of the stockings began to move and my daughter reached in and . . . Do you want to guess what she pulled out? . . . A little yippy purse dog that was wearing a Christmas sweater! It was a Maltese that weighed a pound and a half and was guaranteed never to get beyond six pounds. In other words, my manly dog was more like a fluffy white rat. He literally looked like a fur ball that one of the neighborhood cats had yacked up after eating too much Christmas dinner the night before.

> By the end of the first day, I loved that little yippy dog, but he was a puppy, and it's hard to love any puppy on the first couple nights you have them.

I didn't let the dog's size keep me from treating him like a rough and tough manly dog. I named him "Boss" in order to set the record straight and create the perception that he was bigger and tougher that he looked. By the end of the first day, I loved that little yippy dog, but he was a puppy, and it's hard to love any puppy on the first couple nights you have them. I remember that first night; we decided to make him sleep in his kennel. He whined and cried and continually begged to get out. He looked at us with his big brown puppy eyes as if to say, "Don't put me in here! This is jail!" We realized early on that training our dog was going to be a necessity but it wouldn't be easy. That second night, it was more of the same. The third night, the same thing, but after a while, he finally realized that at night, he was going to be in that cage and he wasn't getting out. He realized that it didn't matter what he did or how hard he tried. It didn't matter if he yelped or whined or pawed at the door to the kennel, when the lights go out, there's no getting out of this cage. At first he tried to get out, but after a while, he stopped trying.

About a year went by and I realized that every night of Boss's life, he had slept in his kennel. After making that realization, I decided one evening to do a little experiment. I told him to get in his kennel and he did, but this time I didn't close the gate completely. Instead of locking the gate, I closed it about half way, to where the door was hanging at a forty-five degree angle, and then I called his name, "Boss . . . Boss . . ." He looked at me, but that was the extent of his response. I decided to take this experiment to another level, so I got a doggy treat in my hand, and called for him again. The response was much different this time. He stood to his feet and began licking his chops. You could tell he wanted the treat, but as far as he was concerned, it wasn't possible to retrieve it because he was in his cage. Then, taking it to an even greater level, I got about five feet from his cage, and I dumped an entire bag of dog treats on the ground. He was beyond excited. He was motivated and moving around, licking his chops, hungry for the treats. He wanted them so bad, but because he was convinced it was impossible to get to them, after a few seconds, laid down in his bed and quit trying. That night, Boss crawled into a ball while lying in his kennel and went to sleep next to a pile of dog treats.

That's a sad story, but what's even worse is the fact that many of us, like Boss, are missing out on blessings in our own lives because we are convinced that we're stuck. We are convinced that we're trapped. We are convinced that we can't change or be changed and so we watch the blessings that God intends for us. We smell the blessings and we dream about them. And for whatever reason, these blessings always seem to be just a little bit too far out of reach.

We've got to believe this today: You can be set free. Freedom is available!

Trapped and Desperate for Freedom

Whatever has you in bondage: that addiction or habit or that thing that's destroying you physically or destroying your marriage or destroying your family or destroying your reputation or destroying you mentally . . . that thing! You really can be set free from it. You can change.

And that's what we've been discovering in this journey through the Gospel of Mark. We've discovered that no matter what the circumstance may be, change is possible with Jesus.

We saw that with the man with leprosy, we saw it with the paralytic. We saw Jesus raise a twelve-year-old girl from the dead in front of her family and heal another lady by her simply grabbing hold of His clothes. We've seen that when we get desperate for Him and when we have that kind of faith—where He's all we need and He's more than enough—that change happens.

> You can't force someone to experience an authentic, life-altering change. Force doesn't bring about real change and neither do facts nor fear.

In this chapter we are going to read about a man who, like many of us today, wanted to change. His story is found in the fifth chapter of the Gospel of Mark and we discover right off the bat that he knew he needed to change. It's also clear that the people around him knew that change was needed in this man's life. I'm sure that those who were closest to him tried to force him to change, but like we've already seen, you can't force someone to experience an authentic, life-altering change. Force doesn't bring about real change and neither do facts nor fear. No matter how hard his family tried, no matter how hard his friends tried, there was literally nothing they could do to cause real change in his life. At first glance, this man appears to be stuck. He appears to be trapped and incapable of change, but as you know already, as long as Jesus is involved in this man's story, there is still hope. Let's read his story:

> They went across the lake to the region of the Gerasenes. When Jesus got out of the boat, a man with an evil spirit came from the tombs to meet him. This man lived in the tombs, and no one could bind him any more, not even with a chain. For he had often been chained hand and foot, but he tore the chains apart and broke the irons on his feet. No one was strong enough to subdue him. Night and day among the tombs and in the hills he would cry out and cut himself with stones. (Mark 5:1–5)

Let's take a look at the time line here. This story kicks off the fifth chapter of the book of Mark. Chapter four closes out with Jesus on a boat with His disciples where all of the sudden a huge storm breaks out. The waves were crashing, the lightning was striking, and the thunder was causing fear in the hearts of the disciples. As the storm was raging all around the boat, it's interesting that Jesus was asleep in the stern of the boat. Jesus was taking a nap. Because of their fear, the disciples woke Him up in a panic saying, "Teacher, don't you care if we drown?" (v. 38). So Jesus awoke and made His way to the top of the boat.

Scripture says that when He woke up, He rebuked the wind and then He spoke to the waves. He told them to be *quiet* and *still,* and once His words were uttered, in an instant the storm was over. Jesus, while standing in this boat, just demonstrated to His disciples what He was capable of once again. And now, they're in the boat, cruising to another region on the other side of the lake.

I'm sure they were still a little freaked out by the storm and that whole experience, and then they were getting out of the boat in a new town and were greeted by this man. The Bible tells us that he wasn't just a man, but he was a demon-possessed man who was screaming at the top of his lungs. It says this man had an "evil spirit," which basically means that this man's life was completely controlled and influenced by the power of Satan. This man had become a maniac because of the satanic influence that was directing him.

Not Your Ordinary Robbery

You may be wondering, *How did it get that bad for him? How did he get to the point where he lost complete control of his own life?* The answer to these questions is the same for him as it would be with us; the answer is sin. Sin robbed him of his own life.

When sin takes over someone's life, it really does look similar to your everyday robbery. I was watching a reporter on Fox News break down the bank robbery epidemic in America the other night. He showed how the downward turn in our economy was leading to a spike in bank robberies in just about every state. As he discussed a few specific robberies, he showed how most of them have a common course of action. He said that the first step of most robbers is to walk in the door like any other customer. They want to blend in and look completely natural. They don't want to stick out in any way, so they will dress in normal clothes and attempt to blend in. But then he showed how the second part of the process would be to scope out their surroundings. After the robber feels like he's blending in, he would then begin roaming around and looking to see where the possible threats may be. The reporter showed that after the first two steps are complete and the robber feels comfortable with his surroundings, that the following step would be an action step.

At that point, the robber would either pull out a weapon or slip the bank teller a note; either way, it would be an action step that would move this person from being someone who was just blending in to becoming the one in complete control of the bank.

That sounds like the exact same way sin works in our lives. Most of us don't jump into the deep end with big sins in our lives, but we often fall victim to allowing little sins to creep into our world. We say, "It's just a little sin. It's not hurting anybody," but before too long that little sin that walked into the front door of your life and looked completely harmless begins to grow. When sin grows in our life and becomes a more dominant

> When sin grows in our life and becomes a more dominant part of our persona, there comes a point where that sin will take an action step and take over complete control of who we are.

part of our persona, there comes a point where that sin will take an action step and take over complete control of who we are. That one-time small sin of lust is now an all-out monster and dictates and determines our actions and decisions. That one-time micro-sin called greed is now a macro-problem and causing us to cheat, steal, and do whatever it takes to acquire more and accumulate much. Sin has the ability to rob us of our life and it's the reason this man was robbed of his.

He Was Robbed of His Sanity

> This man lived in the tombs, and no one could
> bind him any more, not even with a chain. For
> he had often been chained hand and foot, but
> he tore the chains apart and broke the irons on
> his feet. No one was strong enough to subdue
> him. (Mark 5:3–4)

This man was insane! He was mad! He was living in
complete isolation in a filthy place. Scripture says that he
was living in the tombs. The tombs are where they would
store dead bodies and, in many cases, the bodies would be
exposed. If you couldn't afford to have a proper funeral and
burial, the officials would toss your body into a tomb and call
it good. This man chose to live there. He's no longer enjoying
real life in society. He's now living among the dead because
he had been robbed of his sanity.

He Was Robbed of His Self-Control

In school, the day I dreaded most was report card day.
Every six weeks we would get our report cards and we would
be required to bring them home and get our parents to sign
them. Grades were pretty important in our home, but my
parents weren't militant with their expectations. I'm assum-
ing they were more lenient in this area when they recognized
that making good grades wasn't going to be my strong suit.

They didn't waiver too much though. Just because I wasn't going to be a straight-A student didn't mean I was off the hook when it came to my grades. They wanted me to try my best and give a great effort when I went to school and if I didn't, there would be consequences.

My friends loved report card day because their parents were paying them off at home. Many of my friends were getting $20 for every A, so report card day for them meant, "I get to go home and get money!" For me, report card day meant, "I get to go home and get whipped!" The expectation was for me to try my hardest in school and many times I fell short of that expectation.

When we got our report cards in school, on the left side were our grades and on the right side were our conduct scores. My parents were just as concerned with my conduct scores as they were my grades. There would be several boxes the teachers could check indicating how we behaved in the classroom. The box I always wanted her to check was the "S" box. It meant that my behavior was "Satisfactory." But most of the time I would get a check mark in the box right under the "S" box. That box had the letters, "NBSC." To you and I, those letters would be interpreted, "Needs Better Self-Control." To my parents, those letters meant, "Spank your kid and maybe next time he will get an 'S.'"

"Needs better self-control," sounds pretty bad, but if the mother of this guy in Mark 5 would have received a report card with this being his conduct score, she would have been ecstatic! This guy had *no* self-control. He had lost control of his life; he was wild. The man had chains on his hands and shackles on his feet and the Bible says they couldn't contain him. He was out of control.

He Was Robbed of His Self-Respect

I love reading stories in the Gospels because these men were many times writing about the same things. They did life together, which meant that they walked through many experiences as a group. After they lived one of these events, they would write about it, and later these writings would be canonized and be made part of what we call the New Testament. Luke also wrote about this particular interaction and picks up on many of the same things Mark did. He mentions that the man was possessed. He mentions that he was cut up and had shackles on his hands and feet. He mentions that he was screaming at the top of his lungs. But Luke also mentions in his account of this story that this man was naked! When I first read that detail in Luke 8:27, one question popped into my mind. "How did Mark forget that part? How do you leave that part out?" I'm sure he noticed, but it's an interesting observation that Luke made when you think about it. It tells us that this demon-possessed man just didn't care anymore. He wasn't worried about modesty. He had no self-respect. He didn't value his life or his body.

> Night and day among the tombs and in the
> hills he would cry out and cut himself with
> stones. (Mark 5:5)

This man would abuse his body and intentionally cut himself. He would cry out, shrieking at the top of his lungs. He was self-destructing. It was true for him and it's true for us: sin leads to self-destruction. When you first read this story, it's difficult to relate to this guy. After all, he was a demon-possessed naked man living in a tomb with dead bodies. But when you think about it, he doesn't look that different than many of us. He chased sin and as a result of the chase, this man was robbed of everything in his life. He was no longer in control of his life—the chasing of sin led him to a point where a demon was running the show now. We look at him and say, "Well, he was demon-possessed. . . . I'm not demon-possessed." And that may be true. Maybe you're not demon-possessed, but that doesn't mean that this man's story doesn't look a whole lot like our stories. He had a sin problem. He chased sin. And the chasing of sin led him to a destination where he was no longer in control of his life; the satanic voice within him was now in control. He was no longer capable of doing good because of the bad influence within him. He couldn't make good decisions or live a good life because the sin in his life led him to such a bad place. He chased sin and before too long he captured the sin he was chasing.

> He couldn't make good decisions or live a good life because the sin in his life led him to such a bad place. He chased sin and before too long he captured the sin he was chasing.

In 2010, I was in Belize on a mission trip, and while we were there I met a homeless beggar. I actually met a lot of homeless beggars, but this one was different. When I met him, I noticed that he was missing an arm and a shoulder. He was basically missing one-third of his torso. After building up the courage, I asked him what had happened. He went on to tell me his story.

He said that he was literally starving and he was desperate for food. About that time, a couple of teenage boys ran up to him, laughing, joking, and poking fun at him for being poor. But he said one of the boys had an American $5 bill in his hand and kept screaming, "Do you want some money? Come get it!" so he followed them. After following them for several blocks, the boy holding the money threw the bill into the river and said, "Go get it!" The man explained that he was very familiar with that particular river. He had played and fished in that river for most of his life. He had walked across that bridge several times a day as long as he could remember. He was familiar with the bridge, but he had never jumped off of it before. But the man, because of his state of desperation, jumped into the river to retrieve the $5 bill. He said, "When I jumped, I didn't realize that in that particular spot the boys lured me to, there was a twelve-foot crocodile on the bank that was hungrier than I was." He said, "That crocodile took my arm that day, but in doing so it taught me a valuable lesson." He said that the crocodile taught him to, "Never chase anything unless you're willing to accept the consequences of that chase."

This demon-possessed man chased sin and the consequences were much greater than losing an arm. This man was robbed of his sanity. He was robbed of his self-control and he was robbed of his self-respect.

The wickedness in his life led him to this position of becoming someone that lacks self-respect and, in arriving at that destination, he recognized that he also lacked peace. Isaiah 48:22 says, "There is no peace . . . for the wicked." This man was filled with wickedness, and as a result he had no peace.

> When he saw Jesus from a distance, he ran and fell on his knees in front of him. He shouted at the top of his voice, "What do you want with me, Jesus, Son of the Most High God? Swear to

God that you won't torture me!" For Jesus had
said to him, "Come out of this man, you evil
spirit!" Then Jesus asked him, "What is your
name?" "My name is Legion," he replied, "for
we are many." And he begged Jesus again and
again not to send them out of the area.

This guy was suffering from, "Spiritual Schizophrenia."
In one moment, he appeared to be possessed by demons and
another moment we find him on his knees worshipping Jesus.
So the question arises, how could he accomplish both of these
things at the same time? It was the man that worshipped
Jesus, but at the same time, the demons controlling the man
were afraid. They knew what was going on. James 2:19 says,
"Even the demons believe—and tremble!" (NKJV). They
knew they were in the presence of the Son of God.

For me, it's interesting to see this interaction between
Jesus and this man. And the reason it's interesting is because,
if I meet this guy after church on Sunday, I'm terrified. I
would be completely afraid! The truth is that I shouldn't
be, because He that is in me is greater than he that is in the
world, and as long as Christ dwells within me, there's no
demon powerful enough to overpower Who dwells within
me. But if we're being completely honest, that scenario
sounds terrifying to me. But if you'll notice, when this man
confronts Jesus, Jesus is so cool. He stands before this man

and is like, "So . . . what's your name?" He was so cool, and I think I understand how He was so cool: When Jesus met him, He saw him as a man and not a maniac. He didn't focus on his problems, but He looked at his potential.

We may not realize this, but the sin in our lives will rob us of the same things this man was robbed of. It'll rob us of our sanity, our self-control, and our self-respect. It'll eliminate our peace and our hope and our faith and our joy. Sin will rob us of our life if we'll let it. But even if we've been robbed of everything, when we come to Jesus, He sees beyond our problems and He focuses on our potential.

That's an amazing biblical principle that I hope we don't miss. When Jesus meets someone, He isn't so limited that He sees them only in the moment; He doesn't only see us today, but He looks at where we can be tomorrow if we'll place our faith and our trust in Him. If our hearts are beating and our lungs are breathing and if we woke up again today, that's a sure sign that God isn't through with us yet. He hasn't turned his back on us, but rather, He continues to chase us and pursue us every moment of our lives.

This is the same God that took Saul, persecutor of the church, and turned him into Paul, a great missionary and church planter. He can take a Simon Peter, a cursing fisherman, and turn him into Peter, a mighty preacher of the gospel, also known as "The Rock" and "The one Jesus built his church on." And if we would give ourselves to Jesus just like we are today, we would be amazed at what He can make of our lives as well.

This man's story isn't over yet. It continues in verse 11:

> A large herd of pigs was feeding on the nearby
> hillside. The demons begged Jesus, "Send us
> among the pigs; allow us to go into them." He
> gave them permission, and the evil spirits came
> out and went into the pigs. The herd, about
> two thousand in number, rushed down the
> steep bank into the lake and were drowned.
> (Mark 5:11–13)

Jesus instructed the demons to leave this man's body and to enter the two thousand pigs on the side of the hill. Some would call this a miracle. Others would say it was the first historical account of "deviled ham." Bad joke. I apologize.

Notice when these pigs were influenced by the power of Satan, they became wild just like the man was. Once they were controlled by these demons they showed us a vivid example of how sin leads to death when they ran into the water and died.

> Those tending the pigs ran off and reported
> this in the town and countryside, and the peo-
> ple went out to see what had happened. When
> they came to Jesus, they saw the man who had

been possessed by the legion of demons, sitting there, dressed and in his right mind; and
they were afraid. Those who had seen it told
the people what had happened to the demon-
possessed man—and told about the pigs as well.
Then the people began to plead with Jesus to
leave their region. (Mark 5:14–17)

The townspeople had known this demon-possessed man
for a long time. They had known him by his reputation and
by his actions. This man had been demon-possessed and now
he wasn't anymore. He was normal. He was dressed and in
his right mind. This man had been completely changed! He
had finally been set free. He had finally found the peace he
yearned for. He finally had self-respect and self-worth. He
wasn't cutting himself anymore. He wasn't screaming. This
man was sitting down and completely changed.

You would think that the townspeople would rejoice.
You would think they would be celebrating or throwing a
parade in the streets of the town, but it says that they were
afraid.

Not only were they afraid, but then they looked at Jesus
and said, "You've gotta get outta here! We don't want you in
our town anymore. Get in your boat and leave!" You see, they
were afraid and they were angry. They made up their minds
that they would rather have had their two thousand pigs

CHANGE THAT LEADS TO FREEDOM

than have Jesus. They would rather have had the money for their pigs than have a miracle for this man. So Jesus decided to leave and gave them the desires of their hearts.

> As Jesus was getting into the boat, the man
> who had been demon-possessed begged to go
> with him. Jesus did not let him, but said, "Go
> home to your family and tell them how much
> the Lord has done for you, and how he has had
> mercy on you." So the man went away and
> began to tell in the Decapolis how much Jesus
> had done for him. And all the people were
> amazed. (Mark 5:18–20)

We can't forget that this man was human just like we are. He had a mom and dad at home. He had friends that had been waiting for him, and you know they wanted him to change. They probably tried to force him to change. They probably used facts and fear to change him. They probably did everything they could. But they discovered something that we need to realize as well. Supernatural change can only happen as the result of a supernatural God!

When Jesus met this man, his life was in shambles. He was stuck. He was absolutely trapped in a life that was influenced and controlled by the power of Satan himself. This man was in a hopeless situation and for the longest time was incapable of escaping the hell he was stuck in. And in just a moment, he met Christ. And Jesus showed this man that freedom was possible through Him. In just a moment, Jesus showed him that he wasn't stuck in the cage, but that the door had always been open. And because of this man's faith, Jesus set him free.

Do you need to be set free?

No matter what it is that keeps you in bondage today, realize that you can be set free. Maybe you're convinced that there's no hope for change. Perhaps you've been swayed to believe there is no hope for breaking free and enjoying the blessings God has for you. The gate has always been open! The question is, "Are you willing to walk out?"

Perhaps you've been swayed to believe there is no hope for breaking free and enjoying the blessings God has for you. The gate has always been open! The question is, "Are you willing to walk out?"

CHAPTER 7

Open Ears, Open Hearts, Changed Lives

What do you lack?

Several years ago we had the privilege of going to Greece as part of a "Journeys of Paul" tour. While in Athens, we saw the Acropolis and toured Mount Lycabettus. We toured ancient Agora and strolled through the National Garden, but the most entertaining place we visited during our time in Athens had to be the open marketplace. There were shops and stands selling just about anything you could imagine, and the majority of the salesmen were children. There were street merchants and peddlers screaming and marketing to the best of their abilities, and I recognized that the majority of them screamed the same phrase over and over again.

The phrase that these merchants were screaming out is actually a phrase they've been using for thousands of years. In ancient Greece, it would be common to hear the peddlers in a crowded marketplace yelling out this phrase, *TI SAS LAPAY* (τι σας λείπει;) meaning, "What do you lack?" And they would scream this phrase loudly so that all the people in the vicinity could hear them asking, "What do you lack? . . . What do you lack?" The reason they would use this phrase would be because it would naturally create a curiosity that would make those standing by wonder what the peddlers were selling. As a result of their curiosity, they would crowd around the street merchants to see if they had what they were so desperate for, because maybe, just maybe, it was that one thing that they lacked or needed.

> What do you lack? What is that thing you so desperately need? Just about everyone lacks something, so don't feel alone as you answer.

Let me ask you: What do you lack? What is that thing you so desperately need?

Just about everyone lacks something, so don't feel alone as you answer. Look deep down inside, take an inventory of yourself right now, and try to answer that question. *What do I lack?*

I have had many different answers to that question throughout my life. Dependent on the season I found myself in, my answers would tend to vary. If you would have asked me, "What do you lack?" when I was in elementary school, my answer would have been, "Size." Everyone was bigger than me. I was one of the smaller boys on every team I played on at that time of my life. When we would have pickup games at recess, there were many days that girls would be picked before me simply because I didn't measure up to the competition. My brother was two years younger than me, but I can't remember a day when I was bigger than him. I'm pretty sure when he was born he was four foot three inches and weighed sixty pounds. I was always a small kid. Entering middle school, I continued to be behind the growth curve. Being one of the smaller guys wasn't the problem any-more though; the problem now was the fact that all of the cute girls were taller than me. What did I lack? Size. And I thought if I could only grow and get a little bigger that everything would be good.

There were times in high school when I believed the thing I lacked most was acceptance. I wanted more than anything to be popular. Like most teenagers, I wanted to be considered "cool." Other times during my adolescent years I believed the thing lacking was a girlfriend or a better car or nicer clothes. I was convinced that if I only had these things that my life would look completely different.

Once the college years began, the list of things that were lacking in my life began to grow. I lacked sleep and time and square footage in my dorm room. I lacked the ability to concentrate and to make good grades. Looking back, it's easy to see that I also lacked discernment and wisdom when it came to choosing friends and making decisions. In college, my life was lacking.

After I got married, I realized that I lacked money. As a newlywed, I was lacking wisdom and compassion and the ability to multitask. When I became a father, the things that were lacking were sleep and patience and money once again. In every season of life, there seems to be an answer to this question. There never seems to be a shortage of things lacking in our lives. Many times it is easy to identify these things, but on the other hand, there are times when it's more difficult to figure out what it is that we are lacking in our lives.

What is it that you lack right now? Have you truly found contentment in life? Are you truly satisfied? Are you close enough to God to receive guidance and direction and strength from Him? Have you secured peace in your life? Do you have peace of mind and peace in your heart? Perhaps you're lacking confidence or assurance or wisdom or companionship. You may be lacking friendships or community or affirmation or joy. What do you lack?

You see there's a good chance that you lack something in your life, and perhaps it was even on that list. The truth is you can try to change your circumstances and acquire that thing you lack by yourself, but the chances are slim that you'll be able to do it all by yourself. You want to know why? Change is hard. It's not something that's natural or easy for most of us, especially when you're talking about something foundational, personal, or spiritual. It's just not easy to change, and the Scriptures support that.

In Jeremiah 13:23, the question is asked, "Can the Ethiopian change his skin or the leopard its spots?" And then it gives this answer as a subtle reminder, "Neither can you do good who are accustomed to doing evil."

Do you see the phrase, "accustomed to doing evil"? Well, the Hebrew literally translates that meaning "learned in evil." That's saying that we, as humans, are learned in doing evil, which means that evil is a habit that we've learned and mastered after many long hours of practicing.

That's why we have such a hard time changing, because we have mastered evil. We are really good at being really bad.

Here's how Paul said it in Ephesians 4:22–24:

You were taught, with regard to your former
way of life, to put off your old self, which is
being corrupted by its deceitful desires; to be
made new in the attitude of your minds; and to
put on the new self, created to be like God in
true righteousness and holiness.

Previously we've seen how sin has the tendency to rob us
of our own lives. It sneaks in, completely unsuspected and
looking completely natural, but before too long, it takes over and begins to control you from the inside out. It robs us.

> Sin has the tendency to rob us of our own lives. It sneaks in, completely unsuspected and looking completely natural, but before too long, it takes over.

The Bible says that it's time for us to put off the things that are robbing us of God's best. We've got to be willing to put off the nasty parts of our lives if we truly expect to see life change happen!

When I think about things that are nasty, for whatever reason, the first thing that comes to mind is an armpit. Now, you know as well as I do that armpits are nasty. I'm not real sure why God made them so gross, but the fact of the matter is it doesn't matter how attractive you are, it doesn't matter what kind of clothes you wear, or even how good your hygiene is, your armpits stink.

With that in mind, imagine waking up one morning, taking a shower, and putting on a white undershirt. When you put the shirt on, you decide that you're going to wear that white undershirt for the entire day. Your day just so happens to include a five-mile run. After you complete your run, you get home and decide to mow the grass. Then you weed-eat the yard, pick weeds, and follow that up with working in the flower beds for a while. After your yard looks immaculate, you get a bite to eat and then hit the gym, where you lift weights for a solid hour and then do a Zumba class to get in a little cardio before heading back to the house.

> **Question:** At the conclusion of your day, what would be the condition of that undershirt?

> **Answer:** It would absolutely stink. It would be filthy and the stench would be repulsive.

Now the day isn't over yet. That evening you just so happen to have a date. This isn't just a date though; it's a hot date! It's a date you're actually looking forward to and more than anything, you want to give a good impression of yourself because, in the end, you want a second date and a third date and so on. You want this relationship to go somewhere . . .

Question: What are the chances of that actually
happening if you refuse to take off that undershirt and replace it with a clean one?

In the same way, Paul says, if you want your relationship
with Christ to move forward, the way He intends it to be,
you've got to be willing to *put off* the old self (the sinful self,
the nasty self) and put on a new self (one that is like God,
pursuing holiness and righteousness).

You may be asking, "Why is that so important? Why is
pursuing Christ and His righteousness so important in my
life?"

Answer: Because He's the only One that can
give you what you lack and change you into the
man or woman He intends for you to be.

You don't have the ability to change yourself, but Christ
has a unique and supernatural way of changing the lives of
people that are desperate for Him. As we continue in this
study of life change, we're going to take a look in the seventh
chapter of Mark, and there we are going to hear about a man
that was desperate for life change.

If you would have asked this man, "What do you lack?"
he wouldn't have responded because this man was completely deaf. Not only was he deaf, but he also had a speech
impediment that caused him to be unable to communicate.

> Then Jesus left the vicinity of Tyre and went
> through Sidon, down to the Sea of Galilee and
> into the region of the Decapolis. There some
> people brought to him a man who was deaf and
> could hardly talk, and they begged him to place
> his hand on the man. (Mark 7:31–32)

So Jesus arrived in this new area called the Decapolis. The word *Decapolis* is translated to mean "ten cities." Cities like Damascus and Philadelphia and Canatha were a part of the Decapolis. When Jesus showed up, the people in the town brought the deaf and mute man to Him.

> After he took him aside, away from the crowd,
> Jesus put his fingers into the man's ears. Then
> he spit and touched the man's tongue. (v. 33)

If you're like me, when you first read that, it seems really strange. Now, the first part isn't strange: It says Jesus took the man aside, away from the crowd. That move was vintage Jesus. He wasn't there to put on a show. He was there to address this man's need. The strange part is when He puts His fingers in this guy's ears and then spits and grabs his tongue. That just seems a little strange.

But when you think about it, this man was deaf and incapable of hearing at all, so therefore, Jesus wasn't going to just tell him what He was going to do, instead of telling him,

He showed him. Jesus didn't just talk about doing something great, He demonstrated His greatness.

Once again, this is vintage Jesus. Do you remember Romans 5:8? It says, "But God demonstrates his own love for us in this: While we were still sinners, Christ died for us."

He demonstrated His love for us on the cross and He demonstrated His love for this man when He placed His fingers in his ears, spit, and grabbed his tongue. He addressed his problem!

What do you lack? He knew exactly what this man lacked and he addressed it.

> He looked up to heaven and with a deep sigh said to him, "Ephphatha!" (which means, "Be opened!") (v. 34)

Within this particular text, Mark tells us that Jesus did three things: He said that first, "Jesus looked up to heaven." This man might have been deaf and dumb, but he wasn't blind. He could see. And Jesus looking up to heaven was an acknowledgment of His source of power.

John 5:19 says, "Jesus gave them this answer: 'I tell you the truth, the Son can do nothing by himself; he can do only what he sees his Father doing, because whatever the Father does the Son also does.'"

Verse 21 goes on to say, "For just as the Father raises the dead and gives them life, even so the Son gives life to whom he is pleased to give it."

That's why Jesus could say in John 14:9, "He who has seen Me has seen the Father" (NKJV).

So first, He looked up to heaven. Second, we're told in verse 34 that "He sighed."

That's the Greek word *stenazo*, which means, "He groaned a sorrow with grief." What that tells us is that this man's condition broke the heart of Jesus. He was groaning and grieving over this man's condition. Once I discovered the true meaning of this word, it caused me to personalize that text a little bit and evaluate my own life in a whole new way.

I wondered, "When Christ looks upon my life, is He sighing or smiling?" This text shows us that Jesus, the Son of God, grieves and groans over the lives of men and women that are running away from Him. He

> Jesus, the Son of God, grieves and groans over the lives of men and women that are running away from Him. He sighs over the sin-wrecked lives of people today.

sighs over the sin-wrecked lives of people today. When we find ourselves far away from God, He still sighs for us. When He watches us run away from Him and pursue things that we believe are more important than Him or necessary than Him, the Scriptures show that He sighs and groans a sorrow of grief over us.

He sighed at this man's condition. With a grieving heart, He groaned.

The third thing that Jesus did in this story was to say the word *ephphatha*, which means "be opened," or in a more literal translation means to "be released." He addressed the problem and changed this man's life. And you see, this was more than Jesus' prayer for this man, this is His prayer for all of us today: Be opened! Be released!

Be open to hearing spiritual things and be open to pursue Christ. On the other hand, be released of the things that prevent you from pursuing Him. Put on the things of God and put off the old, nasty, sinful self. After Jesus concluded these three things, the story continues in verse 35:

> At this, the man's ears were opened, his tongue
> was loosened and he began to speak plainly.

He was *changed*! Now he could hear sounds. He could speak plainly! The Greek text literally says, "was loosened the bond of his tongue," which means, whatever it was that hindered his tongue from working properly, at once it all came loose and now he was speaking clearly. It was a miracle that would have never happened without Jesus.

My family was hanging out with some of our good friends awhile back and they began telling us a story that we didn't know about one of their kids. Apparently for a long time, their child didn't speak. They didn't know what the problem was. They went to several doctors and had their baby tested for multiple diseases and disorders, but after all of the appointments and after visiting with all the experts, still no one knew what the problem was. Come to find out, after months and months of research they discovered it was because their child was tongue-tied. They made an appointment with their doctor and once they got there, the doctor decided to operate on the child. It was considered a pretty simple procedure. He would open the mouth of their child and then cut her frenulum, better known as that little thing under the tongue. Within weeks after this minor operation, their baby girl was talking up a storm, and to this day they are having a hard time getting her to shut up.

But that's the picture I see in this story. Forever, this man couldn't talk. I'm sure he tried everything he knew to try. He probably visited doctors and got the experts to review his situation, but after all of his attempts it looked as if he would be mute forever. This man lacked the ability to hear or speak, and then in just a moment Jesus changed his life. Now, look at what Jesus said to them afterwards in verse 36:

> Jesus commanded them not to tell anyone. But
> the more he did so, the more they kept talking
> about it.

Jesus, in His humility, said to keep the news private, but their excitement and zeal led them to make it very public. Many believe that Jesus said to keep it quiet because He didn't want people to lose sight of why He was there or what He was trying to accomplish. Jesus knew that once people got wind of what had happened that the attention He received from the locals would be much different. When He did miracles people followed Him to see the miracles. But the reason Jesus came wasn't to perform tricks, it was to answer the question "What do you lack?" in an entirely different way.

You see, people believe if they are hungry, then they lack food. They believe if they are thirsty, then they lack water. They believe if they are poor, then they lack money, and if they are lonely, they lack companionship. And that's the reason that we see so many people trying to change themselves and failing miserably. They fail in their attempts at life change because what they truly need isn't what they think they lack at all. What this man in Mark 7 discovered that day was this:

If life change is going to happen in the midst of my circumstances, then what I really need is Jesus. I need Someone bigger than me. I need Someone capable of performing a miracle in my life. I don't need the natural. I need the super-natural. I *need Jesus*! This man realized if change was going to happen, then Jesus was the one to run to because in the end, He's the only One that is capable of bringing authentic change in our lives.

As the news spread throughout the town about what Jesus had done that day, verse 37 said:

> People were overwhelmed with amazement.
> "He has done everything well," they said. "He even makes the deaf hear and the mute speak."

What do you lack?

CHAPTER 8

Change Fighter

Not without a fight

You have got to love competitive peewee soccer. A couple of years ago, I sat on the sidelines for an entire season and watched my son (who was four at the time) compete in the five- and six-year-old soccer division, and it was great. It was such a great experience that the following year I decided to coach his team. My daughter decided to play on the team as well. We were known as the "Mean Green Fightin' Gators." When we came onto the field, the other team would cringe with fear. We had bright green jerseys and the kids would wear bright green war paint on their faces. We had a team chant that we would yell before, during, and after the game. The kids would scream it at the top of their little lungs,

"Go Green! Go Green! Go Green!" We would always get the funniest looks from people. I think they were trying to decide if we were a peewee soccer team or just a bunch of little people promoting recycling in the neighborhood.

Before I was the coach of the team I can remember being in the stands, screaming and yelling. I can remember enjoying the game but at the same time I would get frustrated at some of the coaching decisions that were being made. The coach always seemed to put his kid in at the critical times of the game and he would pull out some of the better players. I can remember saying to myself, "If and when I coach soccer, I'm not going to show favoritism to my own kids. That just isn't right!"

Well, now that I've experienced both sides, I guess you can say that I've learned a few things about being a coach who is also a dad. It is true that I wanted the team to win each week, but if I'm being completely honest, the thing I wanted most was for my children to play well. Yes, there is a team, and yes, there are other children, but I'll be big enough to admit that my biggest concern was that my children played well. I wanted them to be successful in the game. I wanted them to score goals and play hard. My goal for them was that they would continually grow and develop and change into becoming the very best they could be. That was my goal for my children. That's just the way dads are.

We have a tendency to show favoritism to our children and we want the very best for our kids.

Now, at the same time, I'm also very aware that there's another dad/coach on the other sideline and his main objective and his main goal is to prevent my kids from doing well. He's pulling out all the stops in order to prevent my kids from being successful. He's doing everything in his power to keep my kids from scoring and from growing and from developing or changing. He doesn't want them to get better; he is doing everything he can to keep them from scoring.

Yes, it's five- and six-year-old peewee soccer and yes, everyone is a winner, but when you get right down to it, we want to win and the team on the other side of the field will do everything they can to keep us from winning.

What does that sound like to you? You know what it sounds like to me? Life. It sounds a lot like your life and my life.

Because, you see, God is our Father and whether we realize it or not, He's also our Coach. He's on our sideline. He's wearing the same jersey we are wearing, and you know what else? He wants us, as His children, to thrive. He wants us to score. He wants us to play hard and do well. He wants us to continually grow and develop and change into becoming more like Him. He wants that for us!

But as much as He desires that for us, on the other sideline Satan stands, and he has little devils swarming around us every minute of every day and their main objective is to prevent us from changing. They don't want us to score. They don't want us to be successful. Their main objective is to hold us back and keep us down. They don't want our influence to grow and they don't want our territory to be expanded. They will do everything in their power to prevent life change from happening to us or within us.

> On the other sideline Satan stands, and he has little devils swarming around us every minute of every day and their main objective is to prevent us from changing.

We've seen throughout the previous chapters that God is in the business of changing lives.

Change isn't something that's easy to do. You can't live your life, day after day, doing evil things and thinking evil thoughts and then just decide to do good because the Bible says we are masters of doing evil (see Jer. 13:23).

We learned in the last chapter that you and I have mastered evil after many long hours of practicing evil things, and that the only way to change is to put off the evil things in our lives and then put on the righteousness of God, because in the end, He is the only One capable of changing our lives. He is the change factor.

Satan, on the other hand, is the change fighter.

In Mark 9:14–18, we are introduced to a boy that was also desperate for life change, but no matter how bad change was needed or how desperately change was wanted, Satan kept fighting to prevent it from happening.

> When they came to the other disciples, they saw a large crowd around them and the teachers of the law arguing with them. As soon as all the people saw Jesus, they were overwhelmed with wonder and ran to greet him. "What are you arguing with them about?" he asked. A man in the crowd answered, "Teacher, I brought you my son, who is possessed by a spirit that has robbed him of speech. Whenever it seizes him, it throws him to the ground. He foams at the mouth, gnashes his teeth and becomes rigid. I asked your disciples to drive out the spirit, but they could not."

As a parent, I can't think of too many scenarios that would be more terrifying than this one. This father was desperate on behalf of his son. His son was possessed, foaming at the mouth and self-destructing in front of all the people watching this story play out.

It's interesting that Mark used this word *robbed*. It said that this evil spirit robbed this boy. And just as sin robbed him, sin robs us today. Satan uses everything in his arsenal to steal from us every single day. Scripture warns us about him. In John 10:10 it says that he's a thief that's here to kill, steal, and destroy. But when he breaks into your life, most of the time he doesn't appear to be this roaring lion that seeks to devour. Instead, most of the time he looks like he's on our sideline.

He'll appear to be wearing our jersey and play for our team. He looks like he wants the best for us. It looks like he wants us to have fun, be successful, and be accepted. Satan has a unique ability to appear as if he's our ally when in all actuality he's the greatest foe we will ever have.

Satan is a liar! He wants to seem harmless. From the time we were little children, we've seen him portrayed as a little fictitious man wearing a red suit with horns on his head and a pitchfork in his hand. Satan wants us to buy into that image and he wants us to consider him innocent regarding his intentions. Scripture tells us in 1 Peter 5:8 to "be sober, be vigilant; because your adversary the devil walks about like a roaring lion, seeking whom he may devour" (NKJV). That's the correct depiction of who he is and what his intentions truly are. Satan uses his lies to deceive us and to lead us into rejecting and disobeying the commands of God in our life.

When we walk in the direction Satan wants us to walk, life seems to become easy. But when we walk away from him and walk towards Jesus, it's an entirely different story. You see, every step you take towards Jesus motivates Satan to put up a roadblock and prevent you from changing or growing or developing in Christ because Satan is the change fighter.

> "O unbelieving generation," Jesus replied, "how long shall I stay with you? How long shall I put up with you? Bring the boy to me." So they brought him. When the spirit saw Jesus, it immediately threw the boy into a convulsion. He fell to the ground and rolled around, foaming at the mouth. Jesus asked the boy's father, "How long has he been like this?" "From childhood," he answered. "It has often thrown him into fire or water to kill him. But if you can do anything, take pity on us and help us." "'If you can?'" said Jesus. "Everything is possible for him who believes." Immediately the boy's father exclaimed, "I do believe; help me overcome my unbelief!" (Mark 9:19–24)

In the heat of the moment, the father believes! He believes Jesus is capable of changing the life of his son, but even in the midst of his belief, he saw up close and personal that Satan would fight hard to prevent the change from happening.

He realized that Satan himself, the change fighter, was also the great destroyer.

Satan: The Great Destroyer

There was a powerful Satanic force within the life of this boy and it was controlling him and trying to kill him. Look back at verse 22: "It has often thrown him into fire or water to kill [or destroy] him."

We may not think of our personal sin in this same light, but the truth is that Satan is working through our sin to lead our lives to a destination of destruction. Satan is out to destroy us! He wants to ruin our lives! Every step we take towards God, Satan comes out with guns a'blazing in his attempts to stop us.

> Satan is out to destroy us! He wants to ruin our lives! Every step we take towards God, Satan comes out with guns a'blazing in his attempts to stop us.

Satan is well aware of how his story plays out. He knows all about the end times and what is yet to come. It says in Revelation 20:10, "The devil, who deceived them, was cast into the lake of fire and brimstone where the beast and the false prophet are. And they will be tormented day and night forever and ever" (NKJV). He also knows that "anyone not found written in the Book of Life was cast into the lake of fire" (Rev. 20:15 NKJV). Therefore, he's working overtime to bring as many people as possible to hell with him and the main tools he uses to mislead us are his lies. There's a pattern to Satan's destruction. His lies are designed to lead us into sin, and sin will ultimately lead us into destruction. When Satan senses that our hearts may be changing and moving toward God, he will do whatever it takes to prevent us from making progress in that relationship. He will deceive us, lie to us, and mislead us, just like the Bible promised.

I've seen that happen in my own life. There have been times when I've committed to be more consistent in reading the Bible. I'll sign a commitment card or make a promise to my accountability partner. I'll tell them that it's time to get serious and, beginning today, things will change. What happens next? A roadblock pops up. Roadblocks have the tendency to pop up when we decide to get serious with Jesus. The roadblock of busyness seems to be a common one on the highway we call life. We're far too busy to add another thing to our schedule. Another common roadblock is the "I'm too tired" roadblock. We talk about how hard we work and then we justify our laziness or apathy by stating that we need time to relax and unwind. Roadblocks have the ability to convince us that we're okay when we're being disobedient. That's Satan at work. He will work hard to prevent us from making progress.

Satan wants to kill and destroy any pursuit you may have towards God or godly things.

He's that kind of friend. What kind of friend is Satan? If you were sinking in quicksand, he's the friend that would rush up to you and, rather than help you out, he would pat you on the head and tell you that things will be just fine.

And perhaps you're convinced that I'm wrong about this whole thing. Maybe you're convinced that Satan is powerless against you. You say, "Satan isn't going to destroy my life. I've given my life to Jesus! He's my Savior and Lord! Satan has no power against me whatsoever." We're all entitled to our own opinion, but the truth is if Satan can't ruin your life directly, he'll try to ruin your life indirectly. When he can't have you, he tends to make a habit out of targeting those around you. He begins to prey on the ones you love and those you care about. He's not only out to destroy you, he's out to destroy your children, your marriage, your godly relationships, your positive spirit, and your family!

Luke tells us in his account of this story that this boy was his only child (see Luke 9:38). In Mark 9:21 it says, "Jesus asked the boy's father, 'How long has he been like this?' 'From childhood,' he answered."

That tells us that Satan wants to get hold of our children while they are young. He wants to destroy us and everything else around us. He wants to destroy the good things in our life while they're in their infancy.

Satan is the great destroyer. He's also the great divider.

Satan: The Great Divider

If he fails to destroy you, he'll back up, regroup, and then attempt to divide you. Satan used the circumstances of this boy's condition to divide him from his father.

You'll notice that nowhere in Scripture does Satan make things come together. He always causes things to come apart. He is the creator of chaos. He uses his power to cause division and it goes all the way back to the garden of Eden in the book of Genesis. God had created Adam and Eve and there they were enjoying fellowship with their Creator. Then do you remember what happened? Satan lied and that lie led to sin. Sin entered the world as a result of the lies and deception of Satan. His influence prevailed that day and he divided God from His creation.

> You'll notice that nowhere in Scripture does Satan make things come together. He always causes things to come apart. He is the creator of chaos.

And because of the great divide that took place in the garden through the first Adam, Jesus (the second Adam) came to build a bridge between Holy God and Sinful Man. And that bridge wasn't built with iron or steel, it was built with the sinless blood of Jesus Christ.

Our enemy will divide men, women, and children from God. He'll divide husbands and wives. He'll divide children from parents, and friends from one another. Satan is a liar and he's the *great destroyer* and the *great divider.*

When you look at who Satan is and what he's all about, you can't help but notice that he naturally separates things. He separates husbands and wives and eliminates what was once considered love. He separates friends and causes division in their hearts. He separates churches that were once thriving beacons of light to their communities. He doesn't bring things together; he separates them.

I love that song that says, "Nothing can separate, even if I ran away. Your love never fails." It says, "The chasm [the gap; a wide difference; like a deep hole in the earth] is far too wide. I never thought I'd reach the other side. Your love never fails."*

And the reason it says that and the reason that's true is because it doesn't matter if Satan is a great destroyer or great

---

*"Your Love Never Fails" by Anthony Skinner and Chris McClarney, copyright © 2008.

divider because we serve a God who is bigger and stronger. He is on our sideline today! He is the *Great Deliverer*.

God: The Great Deliverer

Satan can be a change fighter, but that doesn't change the fact that Christ is the Change Factor. Change in your life is possible if you truly believe God is capable of changing you. No matter what your circumstances may look like or how hopeless they may seem to be, they're not unchangeable. Satan can't destroy you to the point where God can't put the pieces back together. God's not finished with us yet. He hasn't completed His work in us yet. And for us to give up hope now would mean missing out on supernatural change happening in our life today just like the boy in Mark 9 got to experience.

> When Jesus saw that a crowd was running to the scene, he rebuked the evil spirit. "You deaf and mute spirit," he said, "I command you, come out of him and never enter him again." The spirit shrieked, convulsed him violently and came out. The boy looked so much like a corpse that many said, "He's dead." But Jesus took him by the hand and lifted him to his feet, and he stood up. (vv. 25–27)

Perhaps you can relate to the posture of this boy. Maybe your life may appear to be completely lifeless. Your spiritual life may look like a corpse. Your prayer life may look like it's without a pulse. You may be a million miles away from God today. And you say, "My sins are too great." You say, "There's no way my life could change."

Listen, this boy looked dead. He seemed lifeless, and Jesus grabbed him by the hand and picked him up. The Bible teaches that if you believe in Him today—if you believe He's capable of that kind of supernatural miracle in your life, in the life of your family, in your spiritual life, in your prayer life, and in your personal life—He can do the same for you.

God is in the life change business. That's what He does and it's who He is. God is creator. He is love. He is gracious and forgiving and patient. He is the unchanging redeemer and shepherd and healer and friend. God is the resurrection and the Lord, omnipresent and omniscient. He is compassionate and our comforter. He's our counselor, intercessor, and rock. He is sovereign and servant and sanctifier and shield. But also remember that He's our father. He's our coach.

It's intimidating to look across the field and see Satan standing on the opposing sideline because you know he's against you and wants to destroy you. It's easy to be captivated by his evil presence in this world that surrounds us and serves as a constant reminder of the wickedness he possesses. It's overwhelming to think about the opposing coach, but it's equally as rewarding to remember who our Coach is. It's good to remember that our Coach in life isn't only the all-powerful and all-knowing God of the Universe, but He's also our Father and He wants the very best for us. It's good to remember that our Dad/Coach not only wants us (His children) to be blessed, but He's capable of making it happen.

Satan is the change fighter, but Jesus is the Change Factor. And as so many stories have echoed throughout the book of Mark, I believe that if we also put our faith and trust in Him and fall desperately at His feet, that He will lead us to life change. And when life change happens, everyone that experiences it alongside us will be left in amazement. God wants to amaze. The question is: "Will you let Him?"

CHAPTER 9

Life Change in Practical Terms

The stages of life change

There was a season of my life in college where the required reading was so overwhelming that I couldn't keep up. I would pick up a book and begin by reading the first five pages or so. As soon as I picked up on the theme of the book, I'd skip to the last chapter and begin to read. The entire time, I'd be praying that this would be enough, but nine times out of ten the author would have written the closing chapter about something completely off topic. As a desperate college student, that was very frustrating. "Why can't the last chapter be an overview of what the book was about?" I would think. "Why can't the last chapter give some practical insight to the book's topic?" I would suggest. Well, now it's my opportunity to make these suggestions become a reality.

If you're picking this book up for the first time and beginning with the final chapter, there's a good chance you think changing your life should be easy. Most of us are guilty of believing the lie that says life change is simple.

I heard a story about a fifteen-year-old Amish boy a few days ago. Apparently, he and his family made their way to the big city and found themselves in a mall. Obviously, they were amazed by almost everything they saw. There were escalators and food venders. There were lights shining and music playing and a merry-go-round filled with happy children wearing colorful clothes. With his mother and sister staring at the merry-go-round, the boy and his father saw two shiny, silver walls, and were overwhelmed with curiosity. These walls would move apart and then move back together again. The boy asked, "What is this, Father?" The father (never having seen an elevator) responded, "Son, I have never seen anything like this in my life. I don't know what it is." While the boy and his father were watching with amazement, a rather large older woman walked up to the moving walls and pressed a button. The walls opened, and the lady walked between them into a small room. The walls closed

LIFE CHANGE IN PRACTICAL TERMS

and the boy and his father watched the small numbers above the walls light up sequentially. They continued to watch until it reached the last number and then the numbers began to light in the reverse order.

Finally, the walls opened up again and a gorgeous twenty-four-year-old blonde woman stepped out of the little room. The father, not taking his eyes off the young woman, said quietly to his son . . .

"Son . . . Go get your mother."

If changing our life was that simple, the world would be covered with perfect looking people, but the truth is life change isn't

> If changing our life was that simple, the world would be covered with perfect looking people, but the truth is life change isn't easy.

easy. The reality is that we aren't perfect and we have things in our life that we know need to change. We know better than anyone the brokenness of our life; therefore, it's up to us to move towards the change we need. Why is that so difficult? Life change is hard and if we're going to experience it, it requires much effort and diligence on our part.

Throughout the book of Mark, we've pinpointed several stories of life change and within these stories we've identified several stages that lead to that change. If we're going to change, it's going to require work. It will never be as easy as snapping our fingers or walking into an elevator. Real life change requires real work on our part and we've got to be willing to put in the effort if we're going to expect real results. You may be asking, "What are the stages that lead to life change?" Let's start from the beginning.

Recognize Our Need for Change

My grandpa used to say, "If it ain't broke, don't fix it." It was his way of getting out of working on something most of the time. For us, many times we look at our lives and say something similar to this statement. We look at our lives and say, "It ain't broken" so that we don't have to put forth the effort in fixing it. That's why this initial step is so critical, because if you don't recognize your own brokenness, you are incapable of taking steps towards life change. We have to identify the areas in our lives that need to be changed in order to take steps towards that change.

There will be many times when you are identifying change that needs to happen in someone else. Perhaps you have a friend or loved one that needs to change and for whatever reason, they just can't see it. As a friend, it may not be our place to show them their need, but rather, to ask God to reveal to them the need in which they have. There will be other times when God uses us in instrumental ways to begin the life change process in someone's life, but we must remember that supernatural change only happens by a supernatural God and we are incapable of changing anyone.

Pursue Change—Be Willing to Walk Toward It

Once we've identified the thing that needs to be changed in our lives, we are left with a big decision to make. Will we pursue the change or be content where we are? I had a friend that smoked cigarettes in college. He was a pre-med student that knew the negative effects of smoking, and yet, he continued smoking all throughout his college years. One day I decided to confront him about it and asked him why he continued to smoke even though he knew it was hurtful to him. He replied, "I know it's bad for me. I know it makes me stink. I know it makes my breath bad and it gives me a bad reputation among my Christian friends. I know all of these things, but the truth is . . . I don't want to quit."

> There are many of us that can quickly identify that thing in our life that should probably change. Unless we want to change, we won't be willing to take the necessary steps required for change.

There are many of us that can quickly identify that thing in our life that should probably change. We know it's bad. We know that the side effects are hurtful and the long-term consequences will be severe, but unless we want to change, we won't be willing to take the necessary steps required for change. Once we truly want to change, our new desire will direct our feet onto a new path that leads us to the destination we desire.

Pinpoint Obstacles That Prevent Change

Once you've begun your journey to life change, you'll quickly realize that the road isn't perfectly paved. There will be obstacles along the way that will slow down or even prevent change from happening. In chapter 8, we talked about Satan being the change fighter. We talked about him using his power to orchestrate chaos in our lives. We saw that Satan is working against us in order to prevent life change from happening in our world. He wants us to fail; therefore, he arranges for obstacles to be in the pathway that leads to change.

My dad was a track star in college. He ran the four-hundred-meter hurdles at Baylor University under one of the all-time great coaches, Clyde Hart. My dad had never run the hurdles until he got to college, and Coach Hart recognized his talent. In his early instruction, the coach warned him about the hurdles. He said, "They're all the same height, but as you run the race you will notice that the hurdles will begin to grow."

In many ways, the same is true within this journey towards change. At first, we recognize Satan's attempts to slow us down, but because we're fresh and excited and moving forward, we barely notice them. After a while, we get tired. We lose energy and our excitement begins to vanish. The obstacles that were once small have now become larger than life and we have to strain to get over them. It's times like this we need to remember what Paul said in Philippians 3:14. He said, "I press on toward the goal to win the prize for which God has called me heavenward in Christ." Other translations say we should pursue, strive, or strain toward the prize He has set before us. We will be faced with obstacles from Satan until the day we die, but if we get into a habit of identifying these obstacles early and addressing them head-on with the power of Christ within us, we'll be prepared to take the next step in this journey.

Constantly Run Away from the Bait

The majority of Jesus' closest companions on the earth were fishermen. Many people would consider that fact a coincidence, but I think there's more to it. Think about it this way: If you were going to try and teach young, uneducated men the truth of the gospel and the power of Satan, who better to teach than fishermen? Fishing and life have a lot in common.

Anyone who fishes will tell you that if you want to catch a big mouth bass, the best type of bait to use would be a night crawler, a minnow, or a rattle trap that resembles a shad. If you want to catch a brim, you'd want to use red maggots or casters or even sweet corn. If you want to catch a catfish, you can throw out stink bait, hotdog wieners, or just about anything else you can find lying around the house. It's interesting that certain fish bite certain baits. Jesus taught His disciples this same principle, but He talked about how Satan lures us into sin and attempts to distract us from making progress in our relationships with God. Satan knows exactly what bait to tempt us with, and he is determined to prevent change from happening in your life.

That sounds scary, but there's also good news. Satan is powerless against you if you stay focused and continually run away from the bait. It says in 1 Corinthians 10:13 that, "God is faithful, who will not allow you to be tempted beyond what you are able, but with the temptation will provide the way of escape also, that you may be able to endure it." So the question is asked, "Will Satan put bait in the water and try to destroy me?" and the answer is a resounding, "Yes!" He doesn't want your life to change for the better. But God gives you exactly what you need to press on and flee the bait that Satan tempts you with.

Stay Alert to Your Surroundings

When you're in full pursuit of life change, it's easy to lose focus. When you fall victim to focusing both physically and mentally on your surroundings, you put yourself in a high-risk environment.

One of my good friends is a police officer, and he talks about this same concept. He says that there have been times when they are in full pursuit of a suspect; the lights are blazing, the siren is screaming, the adrenaline is pumping, and everyone in that squad car is focused on one goal. They are focused on detaining the suspect and nothing else. He describes this "focus" and this "pursuit" and talks about how it can be dangerous to be that focused.

When a police officer is training for this kind of pursuit, they are told to consciously take the time to think about where they are and where they're going. They're told to continually evaluate the risks associated with the pursuit versus the reward of catching the perpetrator.

The truth is, even in the midst of a wild pursuit, sometimes the most dangerous things in that scenario are peripheral. Our surroundings will either hurt us or help us, but either way, they will affect the outcome of the pursuit.

> Our surroundings will either hurt us or help us, but either way, they will affect the outcome of the pursuit.

In this step, it's important to take notice of the things that surround you. Who are the people you are spending the most time with? Are you hanging out in places that point you to Jesus or play to your temptations? Who are the people that are investing in your life and influencing your daily decisions? What are your surroundings in the midst of your pursuit of life change, and are they hurting or helping you?

Go to the Change Agent

In America, when we have a problem, it's pretty easy to look around and find a solution to our problem. If we have a headache, we go to the local drugstore and buy some Tylenol. If we need extra money, we go get a second job. If we are hungry we visit one of the ten thousand drive-thru windows in our town and grab a burger. If we are bored, we go to the mall or play video games online or creep on our so-called friends' Facebook pages. It seems like there's an easy solution to every problem we have.

That's why we get so frustrated when we try to make changes in our lives and fail over and over again. We try to change and we hope to change, but what we discover so often is that we are incapable of changing our own lives most of the time. When it comes to the catastrophic changes that we need to experience—the personal, spiritual, and supernatural changes in life—there is only one solution. That solution isn't a pill or a shrink or a doctor. The Solution is Jesus. He is the Solution and He's the only One that is capable of moving us towards the change we desire. He is the Change Agent, and once we figure that out, we have to make a cognitive decision to move towards Him. With one step following the previous step, we have to constantly move towards Christ. And when we do, we move away from the sin that plagues us and we make progress in the journey to life change.

Be Desperate

When you look at all of the life change stories in the book of Mark, there are a couple of common denominators that connect them all. First of all, every single one of these individuals understood that they had a need for change. They knew that something in their lives needed to change and they also understood that they were incapable of changing their circumstances. Second, they not only wanted change to happen in their life, but they were desperate for that change to happen.

When God's people become desperate, God listens. In every story we've read up to this point, we've seen men and women on their knees before Jesus, desperate for change to happen in their lives. And every time we see desperate people, we soon get a chance to see delivered people.

Desperate people just look different. Have you ever seen a desperate mother? Have you seen a mother whose baby is in danger or hungry or hurting? This mother looks different than your average mother. She doesn't have anything else on her mind. She's focused on one thing because she's only desperate for one thing.

> I believe when we get desperate for life change to happen and we beg God to supernaturally intervene in our world, that He does.

When Jesus looked at these individuals, He saw desperate people and they looked different to Him. I believe when we get desperate for life change to happen and we beg God to supernaturally intervene in our world, that He does. That doesn't mean that He gives us exactly what we want, when we want it, but it means that when we're desperate, we have God's attention and He responds accordingly.

Be Persistent, Consistent, and Determined

When people are desperate for life change and desperate for Jesus, their desperation should be resembled in their prayer life. God calls us to stay on our knees and on our face. Our desperation leads us to be persistent in following Him, but the truth is, most people become more dependent on themselves when they are in the midst of this pursuit of life change.

How can we become more persistent people and pursue Jesus throughout this journey? I believe there are several steps we can take to become more persistent, consistent, and determined people.

The first step is to **set a goal**. We've got to know where we're headed if we're ever going to arrive at the destination we desire. Identify the change that needs to take place, then go to Jesus and beg Him to get you there.

The second step is to **break the goal down into achievable segments.** Sometimes goals can be overwhelming. When you break the goal down into segments, it automatically creates checkpoints that allow you to pause and evaluate where you are in the journey.

The third step is to simply **do something**. You've got to start somewhere. It's important that we take action steps towards change. Identify how you can start and then do something about it.

The fourth step is to **learn what motivates you.** Momentum is created by motivation, and if you're going to experience momentum in your pursuit of life change, you've got to identify the things that are going to motivate you. Learn to focus on the motivating factors and keep your eye on the prize.

The fifth step is to **put reminders up in prominent places.** These reminders keep your goal and your pursuit of life change at the forefront of your thinking. These reminders can be all sorts of different things—anything from sticky notes to reminders on your cell phone—but as long as you are constantly reminded, it allows you to become more persistent in this journey.

The sixth part of this process would be to **make it a habit.** If there's something you need to do every single day as part of your path to life change, it's more obtainable if you make it a habitual part of your life. For instance, if you have lacked a personal time of prayer and you want to make this a part of your daily schedule, it's more doable if you connect it to something you already do on a day-to-day basis. In other words, if you brush your teeth twice a day, you can tie prayer to this event and make it a two-fold habit. And then, when you brush your teeth, you also pray. The same is true for driving to work or walking the dog or getting the mail.

You do these things already. They are habitual. And by tying prayer to a predetermined part of your schedule and pairing the two, it allows you to make this new thing a habit in your life as well.

The seventh part of becoming more persistent and consistent is to **make it fun.** The reason teenagers hate homework is because homework isn't fun. When something is boring, we tend to find ways to eliminate these things from our schedule. Make your pursuit of life change fun. Find ways to challenge yourself and keep it fresh, but no matter what, don't become bored in your pursuit of Jesus.

The eighth and final step of this process is to **go public.** The more people that know about our pursuit of life change, the easier it will be to obtain it. There's nothing more encouraging than having like-minded friends with faith surrounding us and encouraging us in a journey such as this. Jesus wants to change our life, but as we've seen through this study, the majority of the individuals we've looked at had a very public transformation. Their problems were public. Their needs for change were public, and once their lives were transformed by the power of God, the celebrations were public as well.

God is in the life change business, and if we pursue Him desperately and agree to take appropriate steps of faith and action, God will continue to show us that supernatural change in our life is possible.

About the Author

Jordan Easley joined the staff of Long Hollow Baptist Church (Hendersonville, Tennessee) in late 2012 as the first multi-site development pastor, bringing vision and strategy to reach more people throughout Middle Tennessee. In addition, he is one of Long Hollow's primary speakers on Sunday mornings and Wednesday evenings.

Prior to being in Tennessee, he was the student pastor as well as the teaching pastor for the Access service at Second Baptist Houston. Jordan served alongside Senior Pastor Dr. Ed Young Sr. at the five-campus, sixty-five-thousand-member church. Jordan has also served at the thirty-thousand-member Prestonwood Baptist Church in Plano, Texas, and then at the sixteen-thousand-member First Baptist Church in Atlanta, where he was mentored by both Charles and Andy Stanley.

Jordan grew up in the home of a pastor. His father, Dr. Ernest Easley, serves as the senior pastor of Roswell Street Baptist Church in Marietta, Georgia, as well as the chairman of the Executive Committee of the Southern Baptist Convention. God has given Jordan a unique platform to speak all across the country to young leaders, pastors, students, singles, and young married couples.

Jordan is a graduate of Dallas Baptist University (Texas) and attended seminary at Southwestern (Texas) and Luther Rice (Georgia). He is an avid hunter and outdoorsman, a Dallas Cowboy and Texas Rangers fan, a golfer, and full-time husband and father. Jordan and his wife, Audra, live in the Nashville area with their two children, Jailee and Asher.

For more information on Jordan Easley,
the Life Change message, or a
FREE STUDY GUIDE
for personal or group use:

www.facebook.com/LifeChangeBook
www.JordanEasley.net